To my wife Pat

Without her constant encouragement
and ceaseless prayer this book
would never have been written.

Also to

Steven

Lyn

Saffron Ann-Marie
and Carly Jane

No Time to Weep

RON NORMAN

MPS PUBLICATIONS
HIGH WYCOMBE

Copyright © Ron Norman 1989

First published 1989
Kingsway Publications

All rights reserved.
No part of this publication may be reproduced or
transmitted in any form or by any means, electronic
or mechanical, including photocopy, recording, or any
information storage and retrieval system, without
permission in writing from the publisher.

Biblical quotations are from the
New International Version © International Bible Society
1973, 1978, 1984. Published by Hodder & Stoughton

Revised & Reprinted 1994
ISBN 0-9523402-0-8

Printed in England and published by
MERCURY PRINT SERVICES LTD
Wakefield Building, Gomm Road, High Wycombe,
Bucks. HP13 7DJ

Contents

1. A Chance at Last — 7
2. Search for Identity — 11
3. Losing Reality — 20
4. Cheating Death — 29
5. The War Goes On — 39
6. New Faces — 47
7. Invisible Cords — 56
8. End of an Era — 66
9. Broken but not Defeated — 73
10. Abbots Leigh — 85
11. Renewal — 99
12. Learning to Live Again — 108
13. Learning to Trust — 118
14. By Water and Spirit — 129
15. Into the Future — 142

Foreword

Some people find it easy to write about their achievements and successes. For others, writing about personal failure is fine if it hits the headlines and pays well or, if later, they have been able to make a success of things. To write about failure, about the loss of everything, including self-respect, and being incapable of helping yourself, is something else.

For Ron Norman, the early romance with drugs turned sour as they took over his life and a 'hit' was needed simply to feel normal. 16 years were lost out of Ron's life to a pic 'n' mix of drugs, but it was mainly heroin that he lived for.

Prison for drugs-related offences, a marriage that seemed doomed from the start and then to have his children taken away because he and Pat were deemed to be unsuitable parents - all this was the way down to hopelessness and despair. Yet there was no time to weep, no time for life, only time for getting stoned.

This is Ron's story ....

Patrick Prosser, Life for the World Trust

1
A Chance at Last

Monday morning, 14th February, 1983. Clinging on to the shreds of sleep like always. Hoping my wife Pat would get out of bed first and go downstairs to make the morning tea.

Valentine's Day was a big day for us—today we were picking up our prescriptions for the last time.

I rolled over in bed and looked at Pat.

'Well, love, this is it,' I said.

Pat smiled but I could see the fear in her face. We'd said it so many times before, that we'd get off drugs. It was always going to be tomorrow.

I made myself get out of bed. Think positive, I said to myself. Only a withdrawing addict can appreciate the determination it took. Monday mornings had always been a bad start to the week for us, what with all our prescribed drugs being used up by Sunday morning, and Sunday being such a bad day to score.

I turned to Pat. 'I'm going, love,' I said. 'With you or without you.'

'Of course I'll go,' she answered. 'Don't we always go everywhere together?'

True, I thought. We'd been together for the last

eight or nine years, or was it more? It's amazing how drugs distort the memory. Married for around seven years. Married to drugs for longer—maybe sixteen years. Both of us.

Today, Valentine's Day, we were saying goodbye to a long and painful affair with the needle. We were starting a relationship with someone called Jesus—a relationship which seemed to us just as uncertain and fearful as the one we'd had with drugs. Today was the day. We were going to turn our backs on drugs, and put our trust in God and a place called Abbots Leigh, somewhere in Sussex. A place where we'd been told we could get our heads together and rebuild our lives and family.

This God must be some guy if he can do all this for us, I thought.

We'd decided to do it for our daughter Saffron's sake. And if God was real, we had to go for it with all the enthusiasm that we'd had when we used to score. The director of Abbots Leigh told us that if we were going to stay drug free, we needed to get out of our environment. I was still thinking hard about an environment of Christians when Pat called that morning tea was ready.

I went to get Saffron up as usual. It was a shock, walking into her room and finding it empty. Then my mind cleared and I remembered that our friends Alex and Margaret had taken her the night before. Suddenly the reality of our decision sank in. Saffron was going to stay with them until Pat and I were off drugs and ready for her. So much seemed to be happening so fast.

My mind was flooded with fear of the unknown. What did we really know about these Christians? They invaded our lives, took our daughter, and now they were just about to ship Pat and me to a drug rehab miles away. I know we made some kind of commitment to this guy Jesus. But to give up our prescriptions—our script!—we must be insane.

'Come on, Don, it's getting late.' Pat's voice brought me back to reality. I went downstairs.

'You know that prayer we prayed with Alex,' I said. 'Is that really enough for us just to walk away from the only life we know?'

'It'll be all right,' said Pat encouragingly. We sat down looking like two washed-out peanut shells, and prayed together for the first time.

'Lord, we don't really know you, or what Christianity is all about. But thank you for what you've done for us already. You've opened doors we thought were closed for ever. Lord, we're putting our lives in your hands. Please watch over Saffron, we love her so much. Amen.'

It was simple—a kid's prayer. That's how we felt, like lost kids. Then we got up and packed our belongings: they went into one suitcase and three carrier bags.

'Not a lot to show for all these years together, is it?' I said.

'We've got each other,' said Pat. 'Don't worry.' My wife's great—she knows just what to say and when to say it.

We picked up our bags and walked away from all our painful memories; to what, we didn't know.

First stop was the pharmacy for our script. The habit of a lifetime. Quickly out to the toilets to go through the addict's ritual of breaking open amps and searching for a vein. As the red blood mingled with the methadone I felt better, and I had a sudden impulse to go and see our psychiatrist. He'd been good to me and Pat, more a friend than a doctor. I walked to his office humming a song I'd heard years ago from a Salvation Army Officer in London. I scribbled the first lines down on a piece of paper and shoved them on his desk:

'It is no secret what the Lord can do. What he's done for others he'll do for you.'

We said our goodbyes and went outside to where the car was waiting to take us on an incredible journey. We didn't know it but God was going to do some great things for us in the months and years to come.

2
Search for Identity

Looking back now, I see life as a series of journeys. Certain steps lead to new beginnings, and that day when Pat and I stepped into the car, we left behind us part of our lives. We'd known both pleasure and pain. Pleasure in the incredible highs of drugs; pain in the reality of what they'd done to our lives.

Settling into the back seat of the car with my head filled with methadone and valium, I began to retrace the journey so far. How did I arrive at this point in my life? Thirty-six years old, and for years my only security had been my ability to score and to stay on good terms with my doctor. The only stability in life with Pat lay in picking up our prescriptions three times a week. Yet here we were, sitting in a car, leaving everything behind us.

Doncaster slid by the windows. I'd driven this way many times before, in the same kind of reflective mood. Usually I'd been on my way to Armly Jail in Leeds. This time was different. I didn't know where I was going, and I was going by my own choice. It was new, and I was afraid.

The car moved slowly through the traffic, heading

11

out towards the M1. By now I was quite stoned and so was Pat. By the time we reached the motorway the casual chat had faded into occasional comments on the scenery—and motorway scenery isn't a great topic for conversation. I always drift off on long car journeys, but this time I found myself looking into my past.

Was I born to be a drug addict? I don't think so. Or was it all a cruel trick of fate, designed to bring me to this point of decision and change?

I suppose if you want to analyse a life you have to start at the beginning.

Who am I?

I was born Ronald, in Queensferry, North Wales. That's certain, anyway. But being born illegitimate in 1946 wasn't the best start in life. My older sister was illegitimate too—the products of uncertain times, I suppose.

I remember some local kids shouting at me. 'Your name's not Smallwood' (my mother's maiden name) 'it's ...' What was it? Memory fails me—perhaps by choice. But memory holds on to the taunts, the stinging words. I remember them all right. As I grew up there was a constant battle going on in my head: Who am I? Once I got onto drugs it became an obsession, a life of fantasy, often erupting into drug-related schizophrenia.

When I was about five my mum decided to get married, to a guy who was in the RAF. It gave us a reasonable standard of living. But an RAF camp in the early fifties wasn't a cosy, settled place to grow up in. To a kid who was a loner, playing out his own little fantasies, it was a shock. You got introduced to the stark realities of the world at an early age. There was Dad, playing war games of his own—only this time

SEARCH FOR IDENTITY 13

preparing for the ultimate conflict. World events that should have been trivial to a kid were right on our doorstep. When the Berlin Wall went up our camp was virtually under seige.

School. Secondary modern. That was OK, secondary was the way I felt. I soon found shoplifting sprees were much more exciting than school. Even being arrested for the first time wasn't bad, but after the court I was taken to a remand centre for thirteen-year-olds. I guess that place formed my character for my teenage years. If rebellion was the in thing, it was for me. It was only a bit of quick talking by my solicitor and promises from Mum and Dad that saved me from approved school.

Then I set my heart on joining the Royal Navy: but no. Those shoplifting convictions made me ineligible. Once again the world told me I was second-class.

By the time I left school at fifteen we were living in Germany. I had no job, no prospects. But the early sixties were a good time to be young: long hair, pop music, freedom of expression. The youth culture had arrived. I was no different from thousands of other kids, falling in and out of love, learning to be a rebel of rebels, in tight jeans and leather jacket.

In '67 my parents were posted home, but I stayed on for the rest of the summer on my own, watching the Yanks preparing for their global war games. It was there I began to feel isolated and insecure. I often felt alone, as if I couldn't cope with the world. I smoked some dope, did a little speed—nothing out of the ordinary for the times. Eventually I followed my parents home to England.

I'd looked forward to seeing them, but it didn't work out. My life seemed to go in a different direction from theirs. Job, home, family—I wasn't ready for all that. I was stubborn and impulsive. My reaction to problems was always to run away—to run to the security of being alone. One day after a blazing row with Dad I packed my bags, but where could I go? No family, no friends in England. I ran to London.

Somewhere in the back of my mind I heard Pat's voice.
 'You all right, love?'
 'Course I am,' I replied.
How many times had she said those words to me over the years? Her voice was a comfort to me; I felt secure knowing she was beside me.

We were getting near the Nottingham turn-off. In that small distance I'd travelled through twenty-one years of my life. I felt confused. Travelling into the future—reliving the past—could twenty-one years of life be squashed into fifty miles of motorway?

I felt this sudden urge to hold on to Pat, to tell her I loved her. I sat still. I still hadn't come to terms with expressing my emotions. The feeling faded like the miles on the motorway. Travelling into the future with a head full of drugs. A new life in front of me, but the old life still inside me. With the sun on my face I drifted back in a methadone haze into the past.

I arrived in London with nothing. If you do that, either you go under—fast—or you find everything you want. I got myself to Piccadilly, the addict's graveyard. In Piccadilly I could hide, there were hundreds of other young people there hiding too, searching for light and life. It took me four hours to find what I thought I'd been looking for. Methedrine. A powerful amphetamine that would expand my mind, giving birth to fantasies.

What actually happened took me completely by surprise. All the feelings that had gone before, insecurity, isolation, helplessness, frustration, erupted into a terrifying experience of paranoia. My life was transformed by a claustrophobic cloud of clinging darkness. My mind was haunted by an unseen presence which harrassed me continually. I tried to escape by taking more methadrine: the invisible enemy dogged me more closely. The more confused I became, the more methadrine I needed, to try to come to terms with what was happening.

On the streets of London I surrendered my life for the next sixteen years. The door of sanity closed. Drug-related paranoia took hold of my life to such an extent that I was no longer in control. I knew what I was running from. What was I running into?

I stepped into a dark world of self destruction and claustrophobic fear. Something had declared war on me, and the war was being fought out inside my head, in dreams, nightmares and hallucinations. Sometimes I had no sleep for two weeks at a stretch. My body would collapse through sheer physical exhaustion, but my brain continued to work overtime, my mind exploding from the pressure of inward experience. The more methedrine I took, the more detached from reality I became.

What was happening to me?

Drug-induced paranoia symptoms are the same the world over: persecution complex, resulting in a fear of people; loss of identity; fear of the unknown; loss of confidence; delusions of grandeur; reluctance to show emotion for fear of being hurt; total separation from reality. Addicts often imagine they're being hounded, perhaps by the police or people from the past. I don't know why. Maybe it's their conscience at war with their sense of good and evil, right and wrong.

In rare cases paranoia turns to psychosis, where the unreal becomes real. The laws of nature are completely reversed, leaving the addict in a world of his own making. That's when he thinks he's constantly being observed, that hidden cameras are revealing his innermost thoughts to every casual passer-by.

The paranoic drug taker has nowhere to hide, nowhere to run, no one to run to. The imaginary mind-games take over, so that his daily life is filled with a constant inner war.

My experience of paranoia went on for the next sixteen years. I was on my own, cut off from ordinary reality and everyday life. I realise now that I became schizophrenic. I kept a hold on this world only because I had the will to survive, because I wanted to win the war, to overcome the unnatural forces trying to take over my life.

To me, anyone who entered my life was an intruder, a spy, part of a global conspiracy to break my spirit. My only option was to get in first, to manipulate them against the enemy. I felt like an actor on the stage of life, being forced to play a part I was just not equipped to act.

I got to know the enemy. I knew he was there. His hidden eyes watched every move I made, his invisible cameras recorded my performance, even my thoughts. I gave him a name: I called him the Movie Maker.

I took to London like a duck to water. Soon I had lots of acquaintances who showed me the ropes. I found the doctors who would hand out prescriptions for methedrine and driminal like street hawkers selling newspapers. Two pounds would get me a prescription for fifty ampoules of methedrine and a hundred driminal. My life revolved round Piccadilly and Soho. By now speed was the only way I could survive the long cold winter. On speed I didn't need anywhere to live, the streets were my home.

My life had changed completely, and so had my name. People started calling me Don. Donovan was a folk singer in the late sixties, and I guess people thought I looked like him. It gave me a new identity. So what? I thought. My own was never much good. After a while I even began to sign autographs for the poor misguided tourists in the West End—it brought in a little cash to finance my habit.

My search for identity had taken a new turn. Ron had gone, and would not return for many years to come. I suppose this was just another act of schizophrenia, slipping into this new role. London seemed like a goldfish bowl: I could see out, but I couldn't reach out and touch reality. It soon became clear to me that the whole world was against me. I felt I was being used in an experiment to find out how far a man could go before his mind cracked and he ended up as a forgotten face in a mental hospital. Me, I was made of sterner stuff. I'd rather die than surrender.

Not all my time in London was so heavy. Once I was walking from Piccadilly Circus to Leicester Square when I was arrested. I'd already spotted these two guys and knew they were CID. But what really blew my mind was that one of them was an old acquaintance from my schooldays.

My first reaction was that this was a new script by the Movie Maker. He knew all my past, he'd try anything. The last time I'd seen this guy he was in his scout uniform, and I was beating him up. Now here he was, years later, arresting me on suspicion of possessing drugs. It's a strange world.

This is unreal, I thought. Don't take it seriously, it's just a game.

'Ron,' he said. He knew my name—my old name. It was for real. 'I have reason to believe that you're in possession of illegal drugs.' I burst out laughing. It was too much for my scrambled brain to take in. Arrested by a boy scout! I'd never live it down.

Boy scout or not he took me to a police box in Trafalgar Square. Imagine if you can three people in a police box, one of them out of his mind on speed. Actually, I was innocent—I didn't have anything on me. But in between my protests I looked down and saw syringes and needles covering the floor. Were they really there? Real or not, it was enough to freak me out completely. I was being stitched up, no witnesses, locked in a claustrophobic police box with a boy scout and a policeman.

By now things were getting serious; this was no boy scout but a member of the Metropolitan Police Force, with a blue card to prove it. After a while I convinced them I was innocent, but would they let me go? No, now they wanted to reminisce, talk about the old days at RAF Lyneham. Me, all I wanted to do was get away and score as soon as possible. What a session. Why hadn't I seen it coming?

Over the months I seemed to develop a sixth sense for survival, and recently I'd noticed that I had developed what I can only describe as psychic powers, quite common in the paranoic. I often avoided being arrested because something in my head forewarned me. I knew which night clubs would be busted, and kept away, and I avoided streets where my freedom would be at risk. It was great, a new weapon in the war. If I knew what was going to happen I could forestall the Movie Maker. He wouldn't be writing the script any more. I could choose what to do. Now I had the ability to play games with him.

The proof came through a little Irish guy I knew. I bumped into him one day and knew immediately that he was going to be my downfall. Within a week we'd both be arrested for possession. One week later I found myself holding twenty-five amps of methedrine that didn't belong to me. Donegal and I had spent the night getting completely wrecked, and now we set out to sell the remaining speed to another guy.

Someone was setting me up. I didn't know why. I knew I could walk away any time I wanted to, but deep down inside I had to find out if this was all real or just imagination. I had to go on, to overcome the Movie Maker's hold on my life.

We were arrested as we walked up to Charing Cross Station. No friendly boy scouts this time, these ones had uniforms on. Donegal wasn't too pleased. Me, I felt good inside, it was such a relief. I could take on the Movie Maker and win. I had faced the world and the hidden cameras and retained my sanity. Or had I? Two weeks later I was sentenced to six months in prison and taken to Wormwood Scrubs.

3

Losing Reality

When you drift off on motorway journeys the first indication you have of stopping is the sound of the engine slowing down and the gears changing. I wasn't asleep, just what addicts call 'gouching'—you're aware of things going on outside you, but you're totally involved in your inner experiences. It's like dreaming, but you're not asleep. Pat's voice broke my inner silence.

'Cup of tea, love?'

We'd arrived at a motorway service station somewhere between Doncaster and London. Time to stretch our legs, have a cup of tea and a sandwich. We topped ourselves up with valium, too. Then on the road again, and into the future.

Back in the car I looked at Pat and wondered what was going through her head. Nine years and I'd never come close to understanding her. What's the point of trying now? I thought. By the time I get to Abbots Leigh I've got to have all this straight. To live in the future you've got to understand the past. I shut my eyes and turned my mind inward again.

It was 1968. They'd sent Donegal to a mental hospital, me to the Scrubs. Arriving in reception was pretty bad, being locked in a room with seven other guys. Most of them starting sentences of five years or more, and from their conversation I got the idea that prison was a way of life to them. Prison is an occupational hazard for drug users, but it wasn't something I was ever going to get used to.

I was put in a cell with two other guys. I got a job in the prison kitchen, and so my life revolved around the kitchen routine. Up at 6.30 am to bake bread, back in the cell at 4.30 pm. That was my whole existence for four months.

In between times I would lie on my bunk and think. I wanted to understand what had been happening to me, but I never got very far.

These days I work as a counsellor at a drug rehab, and I get to talk to a lot of guys about what happens when you take speed. It seems to be a pretty universal experience—you get high on the speed, you can't sleep, then the exhaustion sets in and the paranoia begins. I moved from paranoia to schizophrenia, isolating myself and trying to find the identity I had lost at birth.

But at that time I didn't realise all this. I never thought other people could experience what I was going through. When my release date finally arrived, I walked out into London alone, still cut off from everyone around me.

I made my way to St Martin-in-the-Fields, hoping to pick up where I left off. But any addict can tell you how fast the drug scene changes—four months was too long. I didn't recognise a single face in the crypt. I felt lost and alone: the war was still going on, on a battlefield not of my choosing. I hadn't won at all. I decided to retreat to Doncaster, to my parents' home. Perhaps there I could come to terms with this new personality that covered me like a shroud.

I'd written to my Mum from the Scrubs, telling her about my conviction for possession of drugs. Like most parents who suddenly find their world invaded by a son who takes to drugs, she was completely at a loss. It's easy to blame parents—childhood upbringing and all that psychology stuff. It's usually just an excuse. If addicts are truthful, they know they just drifted into it, and then found they couldn't handle it. They try something they know very little about, and like the experience; then they find themselves saddled with a new personality totally alien to their beliefs and upbringing.

I guess addicts are masochistic. They know they're destroying themselves, their values, their way of life, yet they go on lusting after the unknown. They prefer the unreal world of drugs to the realities of everyday life. Taking drugs sends them into a helter-skelter world, where they spiral towards insanity, then emerge the next day as if nothing had happened. Then back they go again, becoming slaves to the very thing they thought would bring them freedom.

When I got home it was a shock to my mum and dad. My world was beyond their understanding. Me, I felt as if I'd had a nervous breakdown, and was still having it. Perhaps I'd really been heading for one all my life. Perhaps speed was the only way I could come to terms with my personality and survive in it. Anyway, it wasn't easy, trying to pick up the pieces of my life at home. I didn't fit into my parents' world. I became a curiosity in my own family, an embarrassment: they couldn't talk about it when I was in the room. There was no family bond between us any more. I went to the pub with them a few times, but I always felt I was intruding on their lives. And deep down, there was always one suspicion: were they another part of the conspiracy? Were they acting for the Movie Maker?

In the end the inevitable happened. I started drifting into town on my own, and I soon found what I wanted. Even in those days Doncaster had its addicts, and they stood out a mile. It was a society I felt comfortable in; a life and a personality that suited me. We used to meet in a local pub to share drugs and experiences, and I soon made new friends—Annie, Stewart, Ralph, Bill with his long flowing red hair, and Daisy, so called because of the style and colour of his clothes. They accepted me more for my London experience and connections, I think, than for anything I had to contribute.

So another chapter of my life began. To start with we were continually being thrown out of bedsits and flats, but eventually we found a long-term flat with an understanding landlord. Friends would drop in any time, and if anyone had any drugs they'd share them. Then someone would put on some music—the louder the better.

People used to say that the music in the early '70s was influenced by the drug culture, but I think that was a myth. The thing was, the louder you played the music, the higher your high became. So pop music was music to get high on. You could govern your mood according to what music you played. So maybe psychedelic rock music did sow some seeds of modern society's drug problems. But I don't suppose those early rock bands realised the effect they were having on some young people. To me at the time, music was an expression of the soul—it gave you a spiritual high, achieving oneness with the universe, beyond everyday reality.

Mind you, everyday reality had a way of getting in. One day we heard that Stewart had been found dead in the woods nearby: it was my first experience of death by overdose. It was a shock to realise that our closeness and friendship had been invaded by death. But addicts are adaptable, and even close friends are soon forgotten by the next fix. Stewart became a folk hero among the vast army of young addicts. He'd moved on into a permanent trip; we only talked about him when we were reminiscing about past highs and other shared achievements. I was caught up in something way beyond my comprehension: soon death became an occupational hazard, no different from prison.

In those days our main drugs were paregoric, speed, LSD, cannabis and a little smack. One of the first things I noticed was what hard work it was. Being an unregistered addict was a full-time occupation: from morning to night life revolved around obtaining the next fix.

I'd inject anything—even drugs designed to be swallowed could be dissolved and injected. I experimented with everything, always hoping to find something that would take me higher than ever before. Diconal was one. At the time Ralph had a plaster cast on his chest and the doctor gave him some diconal to ease the pain. He rushed straight back to the flat to try to fix them.

That day was the start of a new era for me. My first

fix of diconal blew my mind: I was addicted to them after my first hit. A gift from the gods. It wasn't long before I was hitting every doctor in town for them.

I soon began to have problems finding a useable vein. The constant use of drugs made my arms, hands and feet swell, and they were covered in sores. It was nothing to spend four or five hours trying to get a vein, and when eventually I did, I'd often find that the blood had congealed. I'd have to drink whatever it was I'd been trying to fix.

As soon as I was back on drugs, of course, the Movie Maker leapt into action. I was aware of him all the time, and everyone was suspect. For example, there was Dawn, a girl I'd been living with on and off for a while. On one particular occasion I'd been up speeding for three days and I was really out of my head. Towards evening I was sitting in a chair in the flat, listening to the Movie Maker condemning my soul. The great lens of his movie camera filled my mind, and the threads of sanity were stretched.

The thing that bothered me most that night was that Dawn seemed oblivious to it all. How could all this be happening without her consent? She must be part of it, I thought. She must have agreed to take part in the play; perhaps she did it for money—actors must be paid. But how could she agree to have her intimate life unfolded on the Movie Maker's screen?

My mind suddenly went into top gear. She doesn't know what's happening, I decided, she's got to be protected from all this. My brain felt as if it was exploding. I knew exactly what to do: I'd have to take her to a doctor. Cunningly I pretended I needed to go to the hospital, and persuaded her to go with me. As we stood at the bus stop people seemed to be looking at us with sad and sorrowful eyes. I could see that they knew what was happening, but of course they'd all been sworn to secrecy by the Movie Maker. Wasn't anyone allowed to help us? Someone out there had taken control of their lives, and was hell bent on destroying mine too.

We went to Doncaster Royal Infirmary, to outpatients, and we were ushered into a room. At first it was hard to get the doctor on his own, but I urgently needed to get him to help Dawn. It wasn't easy, trying to explain to him what I wanted without giving away my part in it all. In the end I decided it would be better if she told him herself, and I withdrew into a corner. I never did find out what transpired between them—we finally left with two mandrex in a packet, apparently for me. Me? It was crazy. It wasn't me that needed help, it was her. I felt as if I was in a Keystone Cops movie.

We went back to her flat and found Jamie and her boyfriend sitting there, smoking some paki black cannabis that had been soaked in opium. I never wanted to miss out on anything, so I was soon stoned out of my mind, or rather restoned. The cannabis hit me like a thunderbolt and mingled with my amphetamine-loaded brain. I sank into oblivion, except I was aware of an enormous weight on my chest which stopped me breathing. There's nothing worse than believing you can't breathe, specially when you're on a depressant drug. My crumbled mind couldn't take it. I freaked out, clawing the air for breath. Dawn said afterwards I was like a wild animal.

They called a nurse up from downstairs, and she wanted to take me to the psychiatric hospital, but Dawn refused; she settled for a lift back to the DRI. So there we were again, only a couple of hours later, in the same room. Only this time there was this huge nurse trying to take my blood pressure. Every time she tightened the tournique I felt as if my head was going to burst. In the end I pushed her away and ran off, straight into the arms of a waiting police officer and a hospital attendant, who carried me bodily up to the psychiatric ward. Ward Ten. I got to know it as The Happy Ward Tendercare Shop. The only thought in my head was that I'd missed out on getting a real tournique—it would have been much better than a tie for getting my veins up. They stripped me and injected me with something or other, and soon I was drifting off into a black sleep.

Three days later I discharged myself.

I thought my dreams had come true when I heard that the local hospital planned to open a drugs unit. If I could get registered I'd know I'd make it as a junky. I was really keen to go and see Dr Wilson, the head psychiatrist of the new unit at the Doncaster Royal Infirmary, but life overtook me.

One night we were all sitting in our communal flat in King's Road, waiting for a dealer from Liverpool I'd met that day. Bill and Daisy were well stoned, Ralph was speeding, and me—I'd missed out on scoring. I'd had an appointment with the employment office so I was out when the others shared out the drugs. The longer I hung about the more strung up I became.

I didn't specially need anything physically, but psychologically I needed to score. Psychological withdrawals can often be more real than the physical ones. In the end I decided to break into a chemist. I headed off into the night armed with grim determination and an old screwdriver.

That was the last time I would see Doncaster for another eight months, because I was arrested coming out of the chemist.

It wasn't being arrested and sent to prison that bothered me this time—it was missing out on being registered, a big stepping stone in an addict's life.

Over the past months my mental stability had deteriorated rapidly, and Leeds prison wasn't the best place to try and get my head together. When I went to Armly Jail in 1972 I was a complete wreck, well on my way to total insanity—drug-induced insanity I'd learned to live with. I was obsessed by the war inside my head, the battle with the Movie Maker. I wanted to do the directing in my own life. I hated the intrusion of total strangers who controlled my actions.

Meanwhile my dreams of becoming a registered addict would have to be shelved. The only positive thing to come out of the whole incident was that the judge who sentenced me sent a letter to the prison governor. It said that I ought to get some help for my drug problem. At last someone had recognised my inward cry for salvation. Someone would help me—or would they?

4

Cheating Death

Every British jail seems the same, a world of poseurs, juveniles, old lags and an assortment of the mentally disturbed. A Walt Disney cartoon land of grey, all mailbags and blue striped shirts. My first night in Armly Jail set the scene for the next eight months. I was put in a small holding cell in the hospital wing, stripped and tied up in a padded gown. They gave me a blue liquid to drink and told me to relax. The white steel doors closed behind me as I drifted off to sleep, contained physically and mentally.

The first thing you hear in prison in the morning is the clang of doors opening and the shouts of 'Slop out.' I got to hate those words over the months. Slops reminded me of pigs, dirty animals reared for slaughter, mindless creatures grunting their way towards the butcher's knife. Was that what I had become?

That morning after a breakfast of porridge and stale bread, I was taken to another cell to wait for the psychiatrist. I was hopeful. Surely a psychiatrist would understand what had been going on inside my head for the past four years. Surely he'd understand my mind games.

At 10.30 am I was taken down to see Dr X who visited the prison two or three times a week. He sat me down and just looked at me, then went through my paperwork slowly and methodically. I felt very tense.

Then he spoke. Words at last, I thought. So he does communicate with mere mortals.

'Well, Ron.' I hadn't heard that name for a long time. 'I have here a letter from the judge in Doncaster, but I really can't see what I can do for you. Are you mad?'

Mad? I thought. Of course I'm not mad. By now I was angry. Mad? I'll show him.

His words just blew me apart. What's the point? I thought. He doesn't understand, he doesn't want to. I'm just another casualty of the war.

The moment had passed. All my hopes of pouring out my innermost secrets vanished when he said that.

'I'll see you every week, but as I've said, there's not much I can do for you. Just settle down and do your bird.' Those were his closing words to me as I was taken back to my cell.

I spent the next two weeks in the hospital wing reliving the past, conjuring up a future built on crumbling foundations, taking my sleeping draught and generally getting bored. When I finally arrived on C wing my attitude was, What the hell? I can take it. The war goes on.

I was tiered up with two guys from Leeds. Life drifted into eating, sleeping and sewing mailbags, and endless chatter about the crimes we'd always intended to commit. The one thing about prison is, it makes you into a compulsive liar and a good storyteller. If a guy was arrested for stealing a hundred pounds, by the time he arrived on the wing it would be a thousand.

Life revolved around if onlys, might have beens, and next times. I told my cell mates about the letter from the judge and the psychiatrist's reactions, but they didn't understand. They'd never been involved in drugs and hadn't got a clue about the Movie Maker and his paranoic films. Perhaps that's why the psychiatrist was no help. How could he heal an illness he knew so little about?

I wanted so much to come to terms with my past so that I could function in the future. I didn't want to come off drugs, just be able to control them. I'd always desperately tried to control my own life, but fate seemed to have played a cruel trick on me. Or was it my inbuilt self-destructive nature at war with my self?

Days quickly turned to weeks, and weeks to months. My weekly conversations with the psychiatrist got me nowhere. He was part of the Movie Maker's army, and I didn't trust him. Still, it was an afternoon away from the mailbags.

Deep down I felt he owed me something. After all, I'd got a letter from the judge, hadn't I? Official treatment was what I needed, but I couldn't influence his treatment of me. I suppose I could have told him about the things that went on in my head—the cameras that recorded my every move, the eyes searching my existence for flaws—but no. That would be playing into his hands and admitting insanity. I wasn't prepared to do that. Go insane, yes. Admit it, no. After all, I was a drug-problem-oriented patient, not a head-banger.

In the end I formulated a plan that would get me official treatment at last. With the help of my cell mates I would attempt suicide and they would save me—maybe they'd even get some remission for their humane deed. We sat down together and planned how to do it. In the end we decided on wrist-slashing as the best choice—after all, I didn't really want to die, did I? Just get them to take me seriously.

The only problem was, I hadn't got the nerve to do it myself, so one of my cell mates had to wield the razor blade for me.

Half an hour after lights out, a shirt tail stuffed in my mouth, arm over the side of the bed. I was surprised how little pain I felt: the first thing I knew was a numb feeling in my wrist. My mates started banging on the door to attract the night watchman. My mind froze. I can dimly remember being carried off to the hospital wing, and watching the doctor stitch up my lacerated wrist.

They put me back in a padded gown and left me in a strip cell—that's a cell with nothing in it except a mattress and a plastic pot for a toilet. Perhaps now I'd get that treatment...I drifted off on the sleeping draught.

I woke next morning to see the psychiatrist standing at the cell door.

'You silly boy,' he said. 'What have you done?'

All my thoughts of Grendon Hall (the psychiatric hospital) and treatment disappeared in a flood of humiliation and anger. Forget it, I thought. What's the point?

Slashing your wrists in prison isn't the best way to get on with people. The other guys think you can't do your time, the officers think you're crazy. Me, I couldn't tell the truth because my cell mates could have been up before the Governor on charges. They never did get any remission off their sentences. And I still never got any treatment.

By the time my eight months were up I'd decided to

go on the offensive in the war with the Movie Maker. I headed back to Doncaster with one aim: to get registered so I could officially be recognised as sick.

Back home the first thing I did was to call on Dr Wilson to make an appointment; I had to get my name down at the new drug clinic at the DRI. Then I went back to King's Road.

By now Bill, Daisy and the others had taken over the whole house. Upstairs was a guy called Jud who wasn't a user but was sympathetic to the cause. Daisy had the flat below and Bill lived downstairs with Dawn. Opposite them lived five Hell's Angels. It was a junky's paradise: I didn't even need to go out of the house to score, unless I wanted to.

'Hi, man, good to see you,' said Daisy as I walked into his flat. It was as if I'd never been away. On his mantelpiece was a little red box of twelve ampoules of methadone and the usual syringe still containing his blood from his last fix. I didn't even have to ask. Daisy went and rummaged in a drawer and gave me two amps of pharmaceutical heroin. I slipped back into my old life as easily as a cartridge into a gun barrel.

I overdosed. The hit blew me apart, my ears banged, my chest felt as if it was caving in, my head went blank. Welcome home, Don.

We had a code of practice for dealing with OD cases. The others would move the victim into the garden or onto the stairs—out of the flat—or else leave him in the room and clear out themselves. Then they'd come back later to see how he was, and inform the police if he was dead.

Fortunately I came round six hours later, on the stairs outside Daisy's door. My first thought was that I wouldn't be seeing Doc Wilson for over a week, so I had to hit the local doctor for some diconal tablets. I managed this and walked away with fifty diconal and a hundred sleeping pills. The sun was coming out at last.

I went back to see if Bill was home, but seeing him with Dawn was painful. I felt hurt and let down—she was still part of my life, we'd shared a lot together. What the hell, I thought. If she thinks she's moved up a league it's her affair.

It was good injecting diconal with Bill. We were soon stoned, talking about old times: it seemed as if we'd been taking drugs for a lifetime. There was something different about Bill, though. He looked withdrawn, his skin pale and his eyes wild. He'd set out to be the number one junky of Doncaster, and by his own account he was well on the way. Yet he was drowning in a sea of uncertainty, unable to cope with his past, present or future. The only way out for him was oblivion.

I understood the conflicts that were raging within him, but I didn't look for the same way out. I wanted to discover the meaning of my life, and I couldn't discover anything from oblivion. I wasn't running from, I was running to something. I wanted to re-arm, load up with speed and go back to war. I wasn't going to be another forgotten casualty.

I found out from Bill that the place to be was the Silver Link, a pub on the ground floor of an office block. I was amazed at the number of people there who remembered me.

'Hi, Don, how's it going?' voices called to me as I went in. I felt as if I was among a family again. I got a coke from the bar and sat down. As I looked around I realised that just about everyone I knew there was stoned. During my short stay in prison there had been a drugs explosion among young people.

Within an hour I'd used up my release grant, spending my last pound on a acid trip. I threw it down my throat and headed off into the night. On LSD I knew I needed to be alone.

For some reason LSD always evoked the morbid side of my character. I feared the night, it seemed to unleash the unknown, yet I would go out into the darkness. I always headed for the graveyard, looking for the meaning of life in death. Tonight was the same. I bent down to touch the gravestones, to feel the power of death over life. A spirit world of oppression surrounded me as I wandered around.

In the end I went home and sat in the empty flat. The flaking walls and dirty windows were suitable surroundings for my mood. I was alone, separated from other people. I wanted to understand this. I needed other people: I knew that I could hide from myself in a crowd, if only I had the courage to stay in it. Yet always I ended up alone. Why?

The next day, fortified with diconal and speed, I signed on at the unemployment office, and once my money started arriving I set about repainting the flat: red and black walls and black and white woodword. Harry the landlord came by with a kettle and some saucepans. Life was getting back into focus. Drugs were plentiful, too: people were breaking into chemists on a regular basis—it was easy to get heroin and morphine. Me, I'd soon be registered on diconal and officially sick. It looked good.

I met Les on the day I finally got a prescription befitting my stature in life: fifteen diconal. I bumped into her on the bus, and she asked me if she could score.

'Why not?' I said, and took her back to my flat. Addicts are good about sharing what they've got.

At the flat I set about crushing up the diconal and injecting her with them. She went out like a light, and I spent the next four hours trying to bring her round. It wasn't according to our code of practice: if she'd died there I'd have jeopardised my freedom, but I didn't think about that.

When she finally came round she asked if she could come back the next day, and I agreed. I don't know why I did: I really wasn't ready for another girl right then. I'd pulled down the shutters on the world and I didn't want anyone else in my life.

I was good at hiding my feelings. When she came back the next day I welcomed her with open arms, though really I was deeply suspicious. Where had she come from, an American, a girl, in my flat? She must be in the pay of the Movie Maker—there were lots of other guys she could have got drugs from. Why choose me?

Les's story was that she'd been arrested with her boyfriend in Los Angeles for supplying drugs. Ronald Reagan was Governor of California at the time, and he was leading a crackdown on drug users. Sure of a prison sentence, Les and her boyfriend jumped bail and headed out to India. They stayed there for about a year, stoned most of the time, tired of life and bored. Eventually they were tempted by the big money to be made smuggling drugs, and set off for Europe with a trunk full of cannabis. They were arrested at an airport in Switzerland. The boyfriend was jailed for three years, and Les was sent to a psychiatric hospital, but later released to go to a relative in Doncaster.

During the two weeks she'd known me, her relatives had found out about her drug problem, and threw her out. Maybe the Movie Maker told them. So here she was living with me.

First thing, I sent her to a local doctor by way of earning her keep. After an hour she came back with a hundred diconal and fifty nembutal. She was all right.

Our life together revolved around sex, drugs and pop music. I didn't trust sex—it made me vulnerable to emotion, and I didn't like emotion—it was risky, it gave control to another person. I had to keep the doors of my mind firmly closed, I didn't dare to open up to anyone else. In the nine months I spent with Les I never did open the doors—after all, she was just an actor in the Movie Maker's script. So we only had sex for violence, possession and revenge. When we did, I felt possessed by dark fantasies, satanic desires. We were always under pressure from the Movie Maker, and we were often violent. At times I got close to going over the top, but I was stopped by the thought of going to prison for life if Les died.

I got Les registered at the DRI too, and our flat turned into a shooting gallery. So many people were coming round for a fix it was like a conveyor belt. They'd climb on, get their fix, and Les and I would prop them up all round the room to recover. I could get other people a hit, that was easy. The worst thing was that it was getting harder and harder to find a vein of my own. My resentment and rage would flare up into violence again.

I'd fallen in love with Les, but I would never let her know. You can't fraternise with the enemy. Outwardly the rows, the blows, the violent sex continued. But there was another problem: for some time now she'd been an illegal immigrant, as her work permit had run out. The obvious thing to do was to get married.

We got a licence and two witnesses and went to the registry office, and the first thing we did was to go to the toilets for a fix. When we finally staggered into the registrar's office we were totally wrecked.

Halfway through the ceremony the guy realised we had no idea what was happening. He asked us if we wanted to carry on, so we said yes, and he made us sit down—it was obvious we were stoned out of our minds. It got worse, then. We hadn't got a ring so I thought we'd use one Les was already wearing, but I couldn't get it off her finger. The poor guy could hardly believe his eyes as we struggled to budge it. He told us just to leave it on and hastily pronounced us man and wife. He was glad to get rid of us.

Living with Les, getting registered, getting married, it all happened in a drugged haze. In the middle of all the confusion, Bill died—not in a blaze of glory as he'd have liked, but on an overdose of barbiturates. He slipped away one night, to wherever dead addicts go. Meanwhile I fell foul of the law again: back to jail, do not pass go, do not collect 200. Three weeks later I was on my way to Armly Jail, en route for Preston Prison.

5
The War Goes On

Here we go again. Through the dehumanising process of prison reception. Finger printed, weighed, photographed, numbered, clothed, poked, looked up into, fed. When you go to prison you automatically see the doctor. Strip to the waist, stand on the mat, tell the doctor your name and number and medical complaints. Quick look through the hair for lice. As a registered addict I was sent straight to the hospital wing.

You can always tell the new guys in prison by the way they dress. If you've got any money or tobacco you can get a reasonable set of prison clothing in reception, but if not you end up with shirts with no buttons, a jacket ten times too big, trousers with twenty turnups or a pair of 1940s football shorts, and shoes and socks that don't fit. I didn't have money or tobacco, so that's how I arrived on the hospital wing. The only good thing about hospital is that you can usually get a single cell.

It's amazing how every cell you go into in prison always needs cleaning. I've never been dirty. Addicts often neglect themselves, but I always wanted to look like a guy who had it together, in control, even if it was only on the outside.

Sleeping draught, clean the cell, make the bed, tea and cake, go to bed. My first night in Leeds Prison—this time round. Leeds is an allocation prison: that means it collects prisoners from all over the surrounding area, and reallocates them to prisons all over the country. At least being in the hospital meant I'd stay there for a while. Once you've been in prison, it's easy to slip back into the day-to-day monotony of prison routine.

Next day I saw the psychiatrist. I could see my file open on his desk—there was a sketch of a hand with a line drawn across the wrist. One more experience in my life reduced to a drawing, and a note in clinical, unreadable, professional handwriting.

The psychiatrist was tut-tutting from the security of his big desk. He handed me a paper filled with the names of dozens of different drugs: the idea was that I should fill in the ones I'd used. With great pride I started ticking them off—I'd used them all and many more. It suddenly dawned on me that I'd done everything that was expected of me as an addict, but I'd achieved very little. The war was still going on without a glimmer of peace, and here I was still talking to this guy who seemed to know what I was going to say before I said it.

Psychiatrists have this way of looking at you, a piercing look designed to bring out your aggression. But often the aggression won't surface, it just festers inside you. Then later it comes out as a fit of calculated rage, known as throwing a wobbler. That doesn't achieve much, either.

In war the best defence is attack, so I burst out,

'You haven't got a clue, have you? You don't know what's happening, man.'

But I stopped. I mustn't go on, mustn't reveal what I knew about the Movie Maker. That would end the war—and the war was the only way of life I knew. Ordinary life was a land that was alien to me, like a country left devastated and barren by years of war. I was a veteran of a conflict that had no meaning to those outside the war zone, but I had to prolong it. I didn't see the psychiatrist again.

Prison isn't the answer for drug addicts. They're full of hopes, uncertainties and fears that rage inside them. Prison just keeps them alive, then releases them into an environment they can't cope with. Prison is a limbo land, where addicts stay until they're released with a handful of money, and then they're supposed to pick up the pieces of their lives—lives they weren't able to piece together before they went in. No wonder the prison population was exploding. Inside it was a controlled environment of continual suppressed hostility, and in later years it began to erupt into large-scale prison violence—but that's another story.

As for me, in the hospital wing of Armly, I was coming to terms with my withdrawal. There was no official treatment other than the old sleeping draught, prescribed for three days only. Withdrawals are a personal encounter, a war between the body and the mind, and I knew the form they took. For me, no surrender, no compromise. To admit I was in pain would be surrendering. So for two weeks I bottled up my feelings, suppressed any symptoms of withdrawal—and retreated into my inner torment. Once again I ran away to solitude, cut myself off from contact, and it only added to my misery, my feelings of being ineligible to join the rest of the human race.

It was quite a relief to move back into the main prison. I began to appreciate having other people to talk to. No matter how much I isolated myself, I needed other people, to talk to, listen to, to tell stories to. The next six weeks I spent in idle prison chatter. Prison talk is all the same—past and future mingle into one in an imaginary world of beating the system, solving the great mystery of where you went wrong. Planning the big one, the one that would set you up for life—a pharmaceutical warehouse or a bank, whatever your aspirations were—it was all played out within the confines of the prison cell. In prison you can plan your future, use your long experience of other sentences, and learn your criminal trade from experts.

For guys who lived locally, Leeds was an ideal prison to do your time in, if only for the visits from wives and lovers. Most of them lived in dread of the daily dinner-time call-up of prisoners who would be shipped out next day. One day my call came.

'Norman, Preston in the morning.'

I spent the afternoon seeing the doctor to find out if I was fit to travel. What a joke. To get out for a day was like a weekend's parole in Blackpool to me. No sweat. I'd heard Preston was a good nick—no more mailbags, anyway.

My state of mind had stabilised a bit, now. I thought that in Preston I'd apply for a single cell and really get down to sorting out my life. It seemed as if I'd spent years trying to do it, but maybe this time I'd succeed.

When the coach drew up to Preston Prison the first thing I noticed was the red brick walls. Different, I thought. Different from the oppressive grey of Leeds and the Scrubs. Inside, the atmosphere was different too. The officers seemed friendlier. Preston is a Category C prison—that meant most of the guys were serving up to eighteen months, with a few finishing off longer sentences. The change of environment filled me with hope.

After three weeks I was allocated to Four Shop, working on sewing machines. Most of the work was government contracts, sort of keeping it in the family, I suppose. Four Shop made fallout suits. Fallout from what I never did find out—they wouldn't have been any good in a nuclear war—but that's what they were and I was making them, at two a week. I was in a single cell on C wing. Full board and two a week seemed quite a reasonable deal for the times.

Four Shop even had its own bookmaker who also ran a football coupon. There were about fifteen other guys there also doing time for drug-related offences, so I felt quite at home, and there were even two from Doncaster who immediately started calling me Don. So I still had my old identity; I got established and settled in well.

Two months into my sentence I received a letter from Les. It was a typical junky letter, full of remorse and guilt because she hadn't written before. It was pretty garbled—hallucinogenic hogwash I called it—but she seemed OK. All the same, I wished I hadn't read it. I'd longed to hear from her, but it brought all the past flooding back in a tidal wave of anger, resentment and unhealed hurts. Paranoia can often lie dormant for months, then suddenly the past creeps up and attacks your sanity again. The single cell had given me time to think. It was great to be alone, but dwelling on the past didn't help. I was back in the depths of pain, failed relationships, memories of violence.

From her letter I could tell Les was still as confused as ever. She was still into Eastern religions, and all that self-enlightenment stuff addicts so often get obsessed with. She was into withcraft, too.

Memory turned back to the times we spent together in a drugged stupor, reading the poetry of Dylan Thomas. Now there was a war hero, a man who knew how to suffer and do it with dignity. I could relate to him and his battle experiences. A warrior of warriors in the fight against the unseen enemy. I thought of his words to his father: 'Do not go gentle into that good night. Rage, rage against the dying of the light.'

When those words started ringing in my head I knew the Movie Maker was still there, able to penetrate even into the heart of Preston Prison. He could search out my soul in the confines of my single cell. The letter from Les was his medium, and now he had restarted the war. Why did the prison authorities let it happen? The whole establishment was in league with him. How could I fight it? I was more convinced than ever that someone out there was trying to steal my sanity.

In a moment all my hard-won balance and calm semblance of sanity was destroyed. 'Rage, rage against the dying of the light.' It became my battle-cry. That night in my single cell I wearily prepared for war again. I was a veteran of many such campaigns, and I knew the enemy wouldn't change his tactics. It started with the voices in my head as usual, recounting my guilt, suggesting suicide. Then reality began to fade away.

My counter attack as always was to try to create my

own reality inside my mind. Make a place of security. I didn't have to make sense of the outside world, rapidly fading away: after all, people don't expect too much sense from a junky. I just lived up to the image I'd already created.

Each night I took on the unseen enemy. Then I had uninterrupted time: I attempted an out-of-the-body experience, taking the battle into the realms of the unknown. It was a battlefield of satanic proportion, where minds wrestled together. It was doomed to failure: each time my dreams of victory evaporated in a haze of mental fatigue, physical exhaustion. Days drifted into nights, nights into days, no surrender, no surrender...

The days weren't so bad because I was with other people. Even the occasional daytime attack from the enemy didn't bother me so much when my mind was occupied by my work. But entering my single cell for the night became a nightmare. I knew what to expect.

It was worse, of course, because in prison I couldn't escape with the use of drugs, as I always did outside. Speed would have recharged my batteries. Many times I was on the verge of seeking medical help, but I didn't want to. If I told the psychiatrist that my life was bugged, that I was being filmed, I might be diagnosed as mentally ill—and that would be a colossal blow to my ego. Anyway, I couldn't confide in the psychiatrist who by his very profession was in league with the enemy.

So my time at Preston Prison, which had started so positively slipped away one night at a time. Every night was a game of hallucinogenic chess played out with an unseen adversary. There were many checks, but no checkmates in the game: somehow I always escaped, or was let off, so that the game could continue.

Every time I went to prison I thought the war would soon be over. But prison doesn't end things, it only takes you to new beginnings. When I left Preston I began to think the Movie Maker was demanding the ultimate price, the death sentence. A fitting end for the life of a crazed junky: to go out in a blaze of glory, a hypodermic passion, a hallucinogenic panic. Like the end of an old black and white movie, holding the hand of the murderer and breathing out a last confession.

Not me. I refused to be party to that. If I was going to die on drugs it would be at a time of my choosing. Perhaps that was the only way I could win.

6
New Faces

Another sentence completed. I hadn't changed. I made my way back to Doncaster, and it hadn't changed either. Everywhere I looked I saw people working, struggling to make ends meet in a declining economy. The other side of life in Doncaster was among the young people trying to come to terms with life through drugs, sex and rock music.

Of the original band who started off on the trail to recognition through the needle, Ralph was living at home registered on diconal; Jock was at home registered on twelve amps of methadone; Annie was living round the corner, still using morphine. Daisy had withdrawn into a world of his own, but he was a real success: registered on twenty-four amps of methadone a day—truly a script to be proud of. Les had moved to London: I was a bit hurt but not surprised. She needed to discover for herself what life was about, and come to terms with it in her own way.

Daisy's was my first stopping place. I knew I could score there, and start again trying to get registered. Daisy showed me a newspaper cutting with his picture and a caption saying 'Don't end up like me.' He'd given an interview, trying to show the reality of drug addiction, but now he seemed to have become a recluse. His life revolved around his prescription and daily visits to the pharmacy.

Every time I went to his flat he was still sitting in the same chair, still living on cornflakes and pork pies, with the same little red box waiting on his mantelpiece.

'Good to see you, man, heard you were out,' he said on that first day. Nothing had changed. As usual, he shared his drugs with me—two amps of methadone were just the thing to blow away the cobwebs of prison life. Then we started catching up on the last few months: five people had died of overdose. All the others were still users, still chasing after the ultimate experience of life, as only a junky can appreciate.

First stop after a fix was to go and see Doc Wilson yet again. Tell his secretary I was out of prison and needed help with my drug problem—actually the only problem I had was that I could never get enough drugs. By now the DRI drug clinic had developed into a maintenance clinic. What a relief: a place to score and swap drugs. A place where I could be kept in the standard of living I'd become accustomed to. Luck was with me: I could see Doc Wilson that afternoon.

Dr Wilson was a product of the times, I guess. A consultant psychiatrist who suddenly found himself doing a job he wasn't trained for. He was continually swamped with addicts demanding more drugs. Often he prescribed out of sheer frustration: how could he deal with a problem his patients didn't want dealing with in the first place?

Doc Wilson was a kind of father figure to me. He was pleased to see me but refused to prescribe anything: I could come back in a fortnight. I was angry and resentful. So I wasn't sick enough to receive treatment? I soon would be. I went off looking to score as soon as I could.

Back at Daisy's I found my old flat would be empty soon—a bit of good news to brighten up my day. When Daisy produced some heroin and coke that was even better news. Once I'd done the business I staggered off to the bathroom to shave off the beard I'd grown in prison.

While I was in there a girl walked in.

'You must be Don,' she said.

Her name was Pat, and she'd met my wife Les at some time or other. She seemed like a girl to get to know: she was registered with Doc Wilson at the DRI, she knew what life was about and where she was going. Over the next few months we bumped into each other quite often, scored off each other and became good friends.

I wasn't really very interested. Life for me at that time was about building a relationship with a needle, not with a person. I had to get sick enough in Doc Wilson's eyes to deserve registering. I was using a lot of heroin and speed, every day, but the trouble was I was always stoned when I saw him, so I never looked really ill. You have to be withdrawing to look suitably sick. Actually I was cracking up inwardly, from using too much speed.

There was a lot of to-ing and fro-ing about what I needed and what he was prepared to give. In the end, after two months, we decided on diconal and valium, as diconal was a lesser evil than methadone or morphine. It would do for a start: at least I was officially sick again. I settled into my old flat again and life seemed good.

I had one last encounter with Les. I went into town on impulse one night and saw her. What a shock—I thought she'd gone out of my life for good. We went back to my flat and she opened a bottle of diconal. We helped ourselves hungrily: we had to get our priorities right. Then we talked. She was living in London with some guy, and she was on her way to Leeds to visit a friend when she suddenly had an impulse to get off the train and try to find me. It was too much of a coincidence for my brain to take. I was glad to know she wouldn't be staying long.

We spent that night trying to relive past times, playing old records, the same old games, trying to recreate what had happened spontaneously before. It didn't work: we'd outgrown each other. We parted the next morning on good terms, she to work out her destiny in other places, me to carry on in the same way, whatever happened. She went out of my life, though how she had come in was still a complete mystery. I never saw her again.

It was on the day that Colin nearly died that my relationship with Pat began to take on new meaning. Colin, like lots of other guys, had started coming round to my flat so I could get him a hit. That morning I was completely out of it, and in no mean mood. I'd spent nearly five hours trying to get a hit, and finally I found one inside my upper arm. The vein was a beaut: I didn't even have time to get the syringe out of my arm before I was in a stupor. By the time Colin arrived I was talking to imaginary people and thoroughly engrossed with things in another realm.

Colin broke the spell. He crushed up his diconal and gave me the syringe to hit him up. I fumbled for a vein—I was good at this, but what was even more of a turn-on was the power I felt when wielding a needle and injecting someone else. After a long struggle for a vein I decided to hit him in the jugular—a first for Colin. I hit him up with six diconal, and he promptly collapsed on the floor. I was really angry: how dared he lie on my floor? His face was pale and his lips blue. Panic set in. What if he died and was found here? I'd be sent back to prison—and worse than that, lose my right to be officially sick.

Fate took a hand at that point. Paddy and Ginner, two brothers, came along to my rescue, and between us we carried Colin out into the garden. It was a better place to die, under the sun. We arranged him as comfortably as possible, syringe in hand, and headed off into town to score some acid.

Four hours later I returned to find Colin still grey and blue, but still breathing. I went up to Daisy's and found Pat there, stoned out of her head on barbiturates and downing some speed to level off her high. She offered to share, but Daisy refused. Me, I greedily gobbled down a handful of pills on top of the acid, and it wasn't long before I was really buzzing.

It was the first time I'd sat down and talked to Pat properly, and I was amazed to find how gentle she was—something I hadn't seen in people for a long time. We talked about her two kids, Steven and Lyn, aged eight and six. We seemed to talk for hours—probably did. We thought of going into town for a drink, but decided against it. I'd become afraid of town, unless I went there to score. I didn't like people knowing what I was, what I had become, and I could tell from their eyes that they knew all about me.

We said goodbye and arranged to meet in a couple of weeks. I was attracted to Pat from the start. She was a person to share experience with, divorced with two children; perhaps I could unburden myself to her. Colin had come round by this time—shame he needed to be told what a great hit he'd had. I pushed him out of the door and settled down to think about Pat.

Of course it all started again—the speed and acid expanding inside my brain, the knowledge that the Movie Maker was in charge. Had Pat been sent like Les, to drift into my life and take what she wanted and leave? My room pulsated like a neon sign—why? Yet underneath, somehow, behind the paranoia, I knew I wanted to keep that date, to see her again.

Pat lived in Bolton-on-Dearn, a village between Barnsley and Doncaster, surrounded by coal mines. It was a different world from Doncaster. Although many of her friends used drugs, they weren't as deeply involved as we were. They were a part-time army, thousands dotted all over the country, people trying desperately to live in both worlds, to use drugs and still live normally. They couldn't cope with either. Work and drugs don't mix, the environments conflict. If you want to live with drug-free people you have to be free yourself; the two worlds are miles apart.

This was the conflict Pat lived with all the time. She was trying to bring up two small children, living with the guilt of addiction and trying to hide it from her parents. It put a terrible strain on Pat. The strain made her need of drugs greater, to help her cope. Yet she managed to be a good mother, caring for the children and keeping her home spick and span.

In most cases like Pat's, the drugs win in the end. But she was a fighter; her upbringing in a coal-mining family equipped her with a determined outlook. She was a good ally for me: her no-surrender attitude was the thing that would bind our relationship.

It was around this time that we met Chris and Liz, two Christians. They were employed by the local health authority and some local Christians on a joint project to help drug addicts. They were great people. They'd shared experiences on the streets of London, and had somehow got off drugs by turning themselves over to some guy called Jesus. It was a totally alien concept to me, but they were good people in their own right, even if I didn't understand them much. They were compassionate, caring, a little overbearing at times, but they had heart, and that's what really counts, I guess.

I'd met some Christians once before, in a place called Orange Street, in London, in 1967. I used the place like lots of others, as a short-term refuge from the streets: tea and gospel preaching were the only menu. I never came away challenged by what I heard of God and Jesus, but rather frightened by the idea of a person who seemed to know exactly what went on inside you. My drugged mind got him confused with the Movie Maker. At the time I put it down to another ploy of the enemy, trying to undermine my mental stability.

Pat and I would often visit Chris and Liz for evening meals. Their conversation centred around Jesus Christ, and I didn't make a lot more sense of it now, but it was good to be welcome there, and they listened when we felt like talking. What amazed me most was the peace I always felt when I entered their flat. They became the people we turned to when we needed help, people who would speak up for us in court. Do gooders, earning their salvation by helping other people, was what I thought at the time. Yet though I used them for my own needs, I respected them for the way they'd got their lives together, and for their giving nature.

As an addict, my life was still filled with highs and lows. Outwardly I was the same person, but inwardly I was beginning to drift into a dark abyss. My fascination with satanic books was becoming more absorbing: to win the war I needed power. I became totally engrossed by the search for power, the ability to control lives through the distribution of drugs. I portrayed an image of kindness and concern for the people around me, and I'd often counsel them about the quality of life and the meaning of existence. I convinced myself that the more people turned to drugs, the greater the understanding of the universe we would have as a generation. The search for meaning and understanding became an obsession. Often my conversations with Chris and Liz ended with me saying, 'The devil I do know. God I don't.'

I know now that the times spent with Chris and Liz were not unfruitful. God was at work in our lives then planting seeds, seeds which the Holy Spirit would bring to life many years later.

By now Pat was spending more and more time with me and less with her children, and her mum and dad had started to take over her role as parent. This put an even greater strain on the family: a huge gap seemed to separate me from her parents, and it often erupted in open hostility. They hated the very ground I walked on. It was just another battle for me: Pat's parents were another tool of the Movie Maker, and they weren't equipped to fight in the same arena as me. If the Movie Maker wanted to destroy me in this world, he'd have to fight with more than just flesh and blood.

It seemed to me that somewhere along the line the love

and peace of the '70s had evaporated into a cloud of anger and revolution. Young people were becoming more and more hostile towards society and all it stood for. The moral structure of life was rapidly eroding, to be replaced by a sense of decay. Me, I was playing my part, willingly or unwillingly. The drugs of freedom had become the prisons of uncertainty, sowing the seeds of destruction in the minds of those who had nowhere to go back to. It was the same for me. I didn't want to come off drugs, to go back to 'normal life'. It was easier to go on than to go back to a society I was alienated from.

I'd come to terms with my addiction, accepting it as part of life. My paranoia, or psychosis, or the Movie Maker, or whatever it was that imprisoned me within myself, was closing around me like a dark secret shroud, leaving me no way out. All I could do was feed the imagination with speed, and hope to come to some understanding of life through a hallucinogenic haze. The prescription of methadone kept the body from becoming sick, and speed would help me cope with my mind, and keep me in touch with the war. By now I'd forgotten what I was fighting for. I'd set out all those years before to change the world, only to find that the world had changed and broken me, maybe beyond repair.

7

Invisible Cords

The journey to Abbots Leigh and a new life was nearing its end. Pat and I were very tired, but the two guys up front, sharing the driving, looked as if they could go on for ever. The night sky was rapidly darkening, and I looked at Pat in the twilight. I was excited, yet fearful. We were going to arrive at Abbots Leigh, that was certain. What the future would hold was uncertain. Yet we'd travelled many roads together in the past. In spite of our inability to cope with life, we'd survived like two Siamese twins, bound together by an invisible cord that had often been stretched, but never broken.

When I started spending weekends with Pat and her kids I often found myself forced to play the father figure. We had many painful experiences there: I failed every time. I didn't know much about being a father. But my relationship with Pat seemed stable enough. We were drawn together by our inner need for each other. 'Children of the universe' was the way I described us, children desperately trying to come to terms with life and with each other.

Pat's home territory seemed to me like a land of giants, aggressive and unloving. I felt as if I was trying to steal someone's favourite daughter—well, I suppose I was. Her parents and her friends disliked me: I was an alien in their community, and I remained one until the day I left. I was an intruder, bringing into their lives a war they didn't want.

Pat's father vented his frustration on me verbally and physically. I was the reason he had an addict for a daughter. Human nature is the same the world over: if you can't understand it, destroy it. Blaming someone else seemed to justify his own inability to cope with the situation life had thrown at him. Pat's family and friends often tried to split us up, but their interference only added to our determination to stay together. There were lots of fights: I couldn't cope with other people's aggression, and I always resorted to violence. Addicts learn this early, because you can't live on the street if you can't adapt to a hostile environment.

Addicts aren't just self-destructive, they're also a destructive force within the family and the community. The priority for the addict is the next fix—and anything that's likely to prevent it is dealt with unemotionally. So the addict has to be callous, uncaring, self-centred.

Yet deep down we all want to be loved, and addicts are no different. There were times when Pat and I went out and we were chased by the local kids, shouting 'Junky! Junky!' Sometimes they threw stones at us. We began to know how lepers felt. To keep the world out, we headed down the abyss of barbiturate blackness, and one day we managed to hit a local doctor for a hundred sleeping tablets each, plus a hundred valium. It became a repeat prescription.

Pat loved to get stoned on barbs. Lots of women turn to drink or drugs, never content till they can find inner peace in oblivion. I guess they feel the hurt more—maybe because of their maternal instincts. They have a great need to love and be loved. Pat couldn't cope as a mother because of her addiction: she hid from that knowledge in a semi-conscious state of barbiturate darkness. She imprisoned her inner guilt where there was no escape, totally isolating herself from the reality of everyday living.

And me, I joined her. I moved in with Pat and we shared the chaos of our lives, stumbling from one crisis to another.

Looking back, I can see I was always running away from Pat, I don't know why. Our relationship had developed into a sort of race on a circular track, with no beginning and no end. The more I ran, the tighter the bends became: I was always coming back to the same place, the same relationship. We belonged together in some way—we were necessary to each other.

One crisis came when she went into hospital with a severe case of hepatitis. She was in the isolation ward of the DRI, so when I'd picked up both our prescriptions downstairs, I went up to visit her. It completely blew my mind.

If I hadn't known her so well I wouldn't have recognised her. Her face was thin, her skin bright yellow, with dark rings under her eyes. She weighed about six stone. I looked at her and thought I was tripping: I couldn't face it. The Movie Maker had gone too far. The girl I loved was nearer to death than life.

I ran out of the hospital, thinking that I couldn't bear to go back while she looked like that. I was filled with anger: how dared he do this? After all, Pat's only crime was that she loved me. The voices started up in my head: 'You're to blame, Don, you're to blame. We don't need her anyhow.'

Battered and confused, I went round to see Veronica—I knew she'd put me up for a while, and Pat's mum and dad would look after the kids. I needed to adjust to being on my own, without Pat. Luckily Veronica's friends had plenty of dope to share, and I spent the next week fixing and tripping out and generally losing myself.

One evening a bunch of us decided to have an acid party. By eight o'clock I'd used up my own script and Pat's, and I was feeling pretty good. There was plenty of speed about, so I indulged myself with some of that, and topped it off with two tabs of acid. As usual, it was one thing too many. The good mood disappeared, and the Movie Maker came roaring into my head like a lion, devouring all logic and sense.

I began to notice that everyone was pairing off. It had never bothered me before, but I'd got used to having Pat around as my partner. I suddenly felt cold and isolated—the familiar feeling of being cut off from the rest of humanity. I knew that feeling of old, and I knew the only way out was to find Pat. She was my security: I felt safe with her. But I couldn't remember where she was, so I stumbled out into the night, looking for her.

The next thing I knew I was standing in the middle of some playing fields, with the rain lashing down all around me. The night was dark, my mind a confusion of helter-skelter colours, fading in and out. The quest for Pat slid into a quest merely for survival. The Movie Maker was hunting me, there in the dark: could I challenge him to combat, could I fight him to the death? The rain became sheets of impenetrable glass, behind which I could see myself as I stumbled around with outstretched palms.

I fell to my knees in exhaustion.

'O God, help me,' I cried. 'I can't fight any longer on my own.' My tears mingled with the rain on my face. I was near surrender—but to what? God seemed not to hear my cries for help, or if he did, his voice was drowned out in the storm raging inside me as well as outside. Lying face down on the wet grass, groping to feel the power of the earth on my body, I thought perhaps creation itself could come to my rescue. I felt as helpless as a child.

My mind turned suddenly to Pat's children, and Pat herself, so close to death. That's what it's really about, I thought. The Movie Maker wants to break the cords that bind us together, he wants me on my own. I climbed to my feet.

'You won't break me!' I shouted into the wind. 'I'll fight you to the last!' I could feel him retreating to a safe distance. Why won't he reveal himself physically? I thought. This can go on for ever. I knew that I wasn't going to submit, yet every time I gathered new strength he withdrew, waiting until I was weaker before he renewed his attack.

The night drew on, filled with LSD meanderings. At dawn I was outside the DRI. I longed to see Pat but I couldn't face it. Never mind, I thought, the pharmacy will soon be open. Breakfast on methadone and another day could begin.

Breakfast over, I headed into town, where I swapped an amp of methadone for two tabs of acid.

Inside my head a voice kept saying, 'Got to keep going, got to keep going.'

I mingled with the people going early to work in the morning sunshine. To start with I felt good, the previous night was just another experience to be logged in the war record. Yet as I walked around Doncaster I seemed to see lots of disabled and deformed people, who gradually began to fill me with fear. Is life so ugly? I thought. I seemed to look deep into people's souls, and saw bitterness, a struggle for life, and hopelessness.

Once again the old isolation crept back. I was different, I had to be. The fear, as always, drove me to quiet places to be alone, hunting for somewhere the hidden cameras couldn't find me.

Just off the Doncaster shopping centre there was a church: surely the one place the Movie Maker couldn't penetrate? I went in and was filled with awe—the roof was so high (was God really that far away?), the air so spacious. The altar at the end of the building seemed filled with a golden acid haze. Peace entered my body for the first time in years, and I felt the presence of what may have been God. My mind relaxed, taking in the splendour of the place, as the serenity of the church engulfed me. I don't know how long I stood, gazing with acid-brightened eyes at the golden aura of the place.

The peace was shattered abruptly by the voice of the Movie Maker pounding inside my head. 'Get out!' it screamed. 'You don't belong here!' My peace fled before fear, and fear before guilt, and I turned and ran. Perhaps I'd made God angry by bringing the Movie Maker into his house with me. At least I knew where I stood: there was no place on earth the Movie Maker couldn't penetrate, nowhere was safe. As soon as I relaxed my guard he was there, waiting to pounce. It was a lesson well learned.

I stayed at Veronica's flat for a while, enjoying what I thought was the good life. One evening I came in to find the flat filled with about fifteen people, all stoned and slowly sinking into their own personal oblivion. They'd been smoking dope through a pipe and lost all track of time. Settling down and piping up seemed the most natural thing to do, so I joined them. Frank Zappa was on the record player, so I let the music infiltrate my body, soul and spirit, lost to the world.

Like always, when things appear to be going well something comes along to intrude, to break into the harmony and shatter the peace. Today's intrusion was the drug squad.

The local drug squad are a very important part of the addict's life. I knew them better than I knew my own parents. Over the years I'd built up a relationship with them: I accepted that it was their job to bust me if they could (which was quite often), but I always felt they had a genuine concern for the actual addict. In some ways they'd become friends, if that was the right word to use. They were concerned at the rate the drug problem was spreading: their lives had become entwined with those of the local addicts, but what they hated most was the dealers. In their own way they were fighting a war, too.

Anyway, suddenly the flat was chaos, serenity turned to panic. The street outside was filled with uniformed police, cars and vans. They were planning a big bust. Naturally we were all arrested and taken to Doncaster police station.

Once there I noticed that everyone was looking out

for himself. It suddenly occurred to me that I wouldn't want any of this lot on my side in a war. They were all running round like chickens with no heads—they might call it self-preservation, I'd call it treason.

Drugs confiscated, statements taken, we were all allowed bail to appear at court at a later date. To me all this was just another occupational hazard, just another frame for the Movie Maker, no sweat. I'd been through all this before and survived. That night was just another passing incident, forgotten by the first fix of the day.

Next day, coming out of the toilets at the DRI, I bumped into Karen and Allen, who lived close to us in Bolton-on-Dearn. They told me Pat had been moved to an isolation hospital in Sheffield, and she wanted to see me. Why not? It was a sunny day, just right for hospital visiting, and I was feeling pretty good.

I went to Sheffield and found the hospital, and was taken up to Pat's ward. Seeing her for the first time in weeks seemed strange: I really had missed her, in a way I thought I couldn't miss anybody. When I wasn't with her it was as if part of my life was missing. The invisible cords tightened and pulled at me: we belonged together.

We quickly got down to the necessary—Pat wanted a fix so I gave her two amps of methadone and a couple of valium. She still didn't look well, but she wanted to go home with me. I'd noticed on the way up that the wards seemed to be full of old people, and she was convinced that she'd been sent there to die with the old folks. If she was going to die, she said, she wanted to see the children first. I was angry at first, then filled with compassion when I realised how ill she really was. Then suddenly I was filled with a selfish fear: what would I do without her? Who would I turn to if Pat died? I agreed to take her home. The nursing staff were hostile, but we persisted and in the end they gave in.

It was strange at first, arriving home together, but we soon settled into familiar patterns. We each got a prescription for barbiturates from a local doctor, Pat renewed her acquaintance with her diconal script, and things returned to normality. In spite of the drugs, and the work of running the house, she slowly began to get better. I called in on my psychiatrist to ask him for the usual letter making my plea of circumstances, because my court appearance was due.

Fifteen people in court made great headlines for the local paper, but for me it was just another disaster. It was sickening, sitting in court and listening to all the whingeing and whining about how all the other guys had never taken drugs before, this was the first time, a one-off. They were all given probation or suspended sentences. Me, I got all the blame because of my long criminal record of drug-related offences, and they gave me eighteen months. I couldn't believe it. Why me? What had I done that was so horrendous that I had to have a prison sentence?

After the anger and frustration died down I accepted it. What difference did it make, in the end? The war went on, it would just be in a different locality, that's all. I'd survived prison before now. Little did I know how much the next twelve months would change my life. I was bound by those invisible cords now, to another person, and that made all the difference. I didn't operate in isolation, and what happened outside the prison walls in those months was going to affect me deeply. I was going to learn a deep hatred for authority, I would be stripped of all my inner hope, I would be left helpless, frustrated, and unable to act when I was most needed in the crises that followed.

Pat was pregnant. At first I was over the moon, but my happiness quickly turned to fear. I realised she'd never be able to cope. Here I was, locked up in Disneyland again, when the person I loved was carrying my child. I wouldn't even be out in time for the birth of our first baby.

Worse followed. Pat's mother died suddenly of a heart attack, and knowing how Pat depended on her to help care for the children, I wondered what would happen next. It was inevitable, I suppose: Steven and Lyn were taken into care. This news just about finished me off. My relationship with the kids had always been rocky, but I knew they were our future, a reason to hope. With the children gone, Pat would hit the drugs even harder than before.

Why me? The Movie Maker had taken everything in the past and I hadn't complained. What more could he demand of me? I'd lost the children, I was separated from Pat, and I was losing hope in the future.

Six months into my sentence the next blow fell. Our baby was born: I had a daughter, she was christened Saffron, and she died fourteen hours later. What else could be taken from me?

I served out the rest of my sentence with only one aim: getting out and getting registered again. That was the only thing I had left. At least I could rely on my prescription, rely on it to take me away and shut out the emptiness of the real world outside.

8
End of an Era

Release from prison held no joy for me. Back I went to the old hostile environment: old friends, old habits, and even older desires. First stop as usual was to score: I made myself extremely sick on the heroin but at least it was a start. Pat had stayed in hospital until my release, so I headed there to meet her. It was a joyful and a tearful reunion. Then Pat discharged herself from the security of the hospital and we went home.

The house seemed cold and empty without the kids, and without the baby we'd hoped for. We would try to pick up the pieces of our past life, but what sort of future could we build out of them? Two days later we both re-registered, Pat on diconal, me on methadone. It was easy enough this time—I suppose we'd both been written off by the psychiatrist as no-hopers, hopeless cases destined to remain addicts for the rest of our lives. Like countless times before, our lives revolved around daily hospital visits, hustling for more drugs, forging prescriptions and generally getting wiped out. We never talked much about Steven and Lyn who were still in care, even less about the loss of our daughter Saffron.

Our home was like a tomb: we had died inside, so we buried ourselves there. Shutting the world out seemed the most logical thing to do, so for two months we lived behind closed doors and curtains, clinging together like shipwrecked mariners adrift on a lonely sea of confusion. Life seemed endless, nights drifted into days, days into nights.

But the pressure of living in hiding was building up inside me. Voices inside my head pointed the finger of guilt at me: the Movie Maker woke up with a vengeance. During this period I became aware of another change of tactics. My paranoia had taken on a new lease of life, and day by day I would sit listening as my life was discussed by a panel of judges analysing my activities, exchanging ideas, and plotting future campaigns.

In my confusion I tried to destroy their plans, utterly absorbed in this unreal world: I was playing into the hand of the one who held me in bondage to the life I was living. My nights were filled with horror, long tortured nightmares, from which I awoke ready to die, defeated by the Movie Maker. But like all dreams, they faded with the daylight and the everyday realities of life.

Early one evening I decided that enough was enough. Pat and I would go for a walk round our housing estate. Stuff the world, if they couldn't accept us for who we were that was their problem. As we went out I was filled with a sudden sense of achievement. I wasn't defeated yet. It was a fine evening. With every step I felt a surge of new life, the will to live flooding back: I was going to fight on.

Now that we'd got a new lease of life we decided to have a party, a sort of coming-out party. Pat invited some of her friends, and I invited Daisy from Doncaster, my reliable old mate from the King's Road days. It was a typical junky party, swapping drugs and getting stoned, music turned up full blast and everybody completely wasted. Daisy stayed over that night so we could all go together to the hospital for our scripts the next day. We had time to reminisce: I hadn't talked to him for a long while. In the morning we left Daisy in the town so he could call in at his flat, and arranged to meet him later.

Daisy never made it to the pharmacy, though he did make the hospital. Walking to the bus stop he had a barbiturate fit, similar to an epileptic fit, and fell through a shop window. He ended up in a coma, fighting for his life.

However, after two weeks of care and attention he came out of hospital looking like a new man, his prescription of twenty-four amps of methadone reduced to twelve. He seemed to have found the will to live at last. We left him in good spirits that evening: after all, not many addicts really wanted to get off drugs, or even knew how to. Daisy seemed a changed man, at peace with the world and himself.

Daisy died that evening. Someone came round to his flat and Daisy succumbed to the temptation of his past. He injected heroin into a system that could no longer take it. Or had someone out there realised that he was no longer useful to them now he wanted to escape? I'll never know. Perhaps he had written his own epitaph all those years ago in the headline in the evening paper: 'Don't end up like me.'

With Daisy's death the final chapter of 27 King's Road came to an abrupt end—that house where so many of us entered the war, filled with youthful enthusiasm and a desire to take from life more than life was prepared to give us. It became a shadow in a memory, a cornerstone of our experience of the life-changing, drug-induced darkness. Daisy had been a local legend, but his death was just another statistic of the war. Those close to him remembered him fondly— a good guy to get stoned with.

Now Daisy was gone, my links with Doncaster ended. For me it became a hospital, a psychiatrist and a place to score. It was the end of an era. Within the drug circles of Doncaster a new breed of addicts was emerging: I called them hippy mutants, because they had no desire whatever for the love and peace that attracted us in the late sixties. They would fester and grow and later emerge on the streets as such a destructive force that society out of fear would isolate them in the ghettoes of the '80s. I could see it coming, and I could see it was the handiwork of the Movie Maker.

In the following years came death upon death. My wife Les died in London from an overdose of barbiturates. Mel died injecting himself with bleach. Dave headed up the M1 only to die in a car crash two hundred yards from his new home. Gary surrendered to a fix of diconal and Julie took her own life, alone in a shabby bedsit.

That's just a few of them, but my memory of death stretches too far back to be any use to life. They were all good people to share experiences with, and they'd all fallen in the war. They wouldn't be remembered as veterans, they wouldn't get any medals, no one even knew their names any more.

As for me, life was still a battle. Pat and I moved into 1976 grasping for new hope. Pat was pregnant again, and this time I would be around to take care of her, and to protect the unborn child. We prepared for the birth like any other couple. I decided that I didn't want my child to come into the world illegitimate, like me, so we decided to get married.

Although the marriage and the baby were important to us, we were still using drugs in a big way. Me, I was still as paranoid as ever, still topping up my prescribed drugs with speed. As the prospect of fatherhood approached, my fears loomed larger, and I went through a phase of barricading myself in the bedroom at night. Often I felt the presence of something outside the door, something alien and frightening. It communicated with me inside my head, always destroying any logic or peace that I managed to achieve. I was still a puppet, forced to dance to the Movie Maker's tune.

There were times when I was grateful to my Creator for installing in me the will to survive. It was only that, along with Pat's constant assurance that everything would turn out to the good, that kept total insanity at bay. I would have surrendered many times if it hadn't been for Pat.

Summer arrived. Pat was six months gone and quite big, and we arranged to get married at Doncaster registry office. On 19th July we set out, picked up our prescriptions and called in on Alan, the best man. We must have looked a sight as we gathered for the ceremony: Pat with her bulge, me in a borrowed suit propping up Alan, and all of us stoned out of our minds. We were so confused the poor registrar nearly married Pat to Alan.

It wasn't much of a ceremony, a quick conveyor belt of 'I do's, but I felt good that we'd got married before the baby came. I began to feel more hopeful: perhaps the birth of the baby would end the long nightmare.

Perhaps one day I'd wake up to find a guy knocking at the door to give me a medal for surviving the war. What a dream. Life is reality, and I was living in the real world. The birth of our daughter Carly Jane was real.

At home we'd bought or stolen all the things we needed for the baby. Pat went into hospital six weeks before the baby was due, and I visited every day. October came, and on an evening visit the nurse told me Carly had been born. At first I thought she was having me on, Pat still looked so big, but that was just my ignorance.

I looked in the incubator and there was the most beautiful baby girl I'd ever seen. It was incredible: they even let me feed her. I couldn't believe how tiny and vulnerable she was.

Fourteen days later Pat was discharged, so we went home to prepare for Carly's homecoming. Our daily trips to the hospital went on for weeks, and still she wasn't allowed home. We should have sensed then that something was wrong.

One day when we called in to see her, Carly wasn't there. First we felt panic, then fear. Then anger and resentment when they told us what had happened: Carly had been taken into care without our knowledge. Our joy and dreams for the future turned sour. We walked out of the hospital more dead than alive, hand in hand, with tears rolling down our cheeks.

I couldn't console Pat, and in my anger I started blaming her for losing Steven and Lyn to the authorities first. Then I turned from Pat to the Movie Maker: it was another ploy of his to break me.

Carly Jane had been placed in the care of a young couple who lived about five miles from us, and once a week we were allowed to visit her at the local council offices. There's nothing more pitiful than to watch a mother playing with her baby, knowing that someone else is acting as parent. It was too much for me, and I switched off to love her from a distance. Eventually it grew too much for Pat, and our visits became less frequent. We stopped building an imaginary future of reconciliation: it never happened. Five years later Carly Jane was legally adopted by her foster parents.

Our lifestyle of addiction had started to touch others: now we had three children in care. Perhaps it was the best thing for Carly—only time can tell. What we did know was that we had been robbed yet again of any hope in the future, by the removal of Carly Jane. We had loved her so dearly. Being addicts wasn't only destroying our lives, it was taking from us a basic human right: to raise children and enjoy life as a family.

Too many deaths, and even birth couldn't bring life into our world. Our friends were dying, our children were taken away from us. We were alone again, with only drugs to sustain us.

9

Broken but not Defeated

The writing on the road sign said 'Haywards Heath 11 miles'. By now it was completely dark, and only the lights of the oncoming vehicles kept me awake. Pat nestled her head on my shoulder and asked where we were, but I never answered. I was beginning to feel agitated: perhaps this was all a mistake. After all, who were these people we were handing over our lives to? Perhaps the Movie Maker was in charge of them, too—we'd soon know. Then my thoughts turned to our daughter Saffron. I missed her already.

When we knew Pat was pregnant again, it seemed like we'd been given yet another chance. The baby was a girl, so we decided to call her Saffron, after our first child who died. It was as if she was being restored to us.

Saffron Anne-Marie was born on 4th December 1978. The two years between her birth and that of Carly Jane had drifted by uneventfully, as we accepted whatever life threw at us. At the time of Saffron's birth our situation hadn't changed, and our new hopes were mixed with old fears. The fears proved justified: Saffron was placed under a care order at birth.

I could only imagine what it did to Pat. Me, I was prepared as ever to go down fighting. At least this time it wasn't the old unseen enemy, but a real, physical one: the Social Services. I wasn't accepting this as fate.

For six weeks we attended the same Social Services office as we had done with Carly. Watching Pat going through it all again and slowly breaking up inside, it would have been easy to give up, to run away from the hurt. I cried silently, for outward tears wouldn't come. Those weekly visits left me a broken man. I'd fought so hard, for so long, and I'd achieved nothing. My memory was littered with shell holes where I'd stood in the minefield of my past. All that was left was to go on, yet there was still a flicker of the old fire burning deep inside me, and my feelings for Saffron fanned those embers into a blaze.

We were summoned to court to explain to a total stranger why we wanted our daughter back. What angered me most was the fact that other parents didn't have to attend courts to show their suitability: why should I? In my mind I was no different from any other father. Had my addiction changed me so much?

To our total amazement (and the astonishment of the Social Services) Saffron was placed on a supervision order for three years and allowed to come home. A new dawn, a new beginning. Someone had smiled on us at last.

Suddenly our lives were full of joy and expectation again—and also a quiet fear. Could we really cope? But we were determined to manage. From that day Saffron would go everywhere with us: our lives would be centered around her. I'd never seen Pat so happy:

she was hoping that one day we might be allowed to have Steven and Lyn home, too. So we started out again—still addicts, but now we were parents, too.

Lots of people know it's not easy, bringing up children on Social Security payments. It's even harder if you've got a drug habit to feed, too. It wasn't long before we ran into debt, and found we had a huge electricity bill of £120. There was no way we could pay, so our electricity was cut off in mid-winter, leaving us with no heating or cooking facilities. Once again I'd failed as a father, I couldn't even provide the basic needs of my family.

We started moving from one friend's house to another, staying till our drugs ran out or they got fed up with us. One evening when we'd been staying with John and Jane the usual happened: they told us we'd have to go. The trouble was, there was a snowstorm and all the buses had stopped running. I tried a couple of other friends but no one would take us in. There was nothing for it but to go home.

We set off for Bolton-on-Dearn in a raging blizzard, and got home to a dark and freezing house. We made up a damp bed and snuggled down together, all three of us, under the blankets. That night I cried from sheer helplessness. Every time things started to get better, they got worse again. I don't know how we survived that night, but we did.

Two months later we moved into a rented house in Doncaster. The house helped, but of course I was back in my old environment, rubbing shoulders with all my old contacts, slipping back into the old ways. It wasn't long before our house was filled with people either stoned or wanting to score. Our life had gone in a complete circle. I knew what would inevitably happen, but I seemed powerless to stop it.

In January 1982 I was back in prison on remand. Pat had a complete nervous breakdown and was admitted to the DRI. Saffron was taken into care. Once again I'd lost: separated from the ones I loved, separated from reality, the tidal wave of disaster threatening my sanity. Why was I such a failure?

The only difference in Leeds prison this time was that they never put me in the hospital wing. I was banged up with an alcoholic and a young guy who played his radio all day. For seven days I put up with it: the continual junk music, and the alcoholic being sick in the bucket we used as a toilet.

My withdrawals were bad, and I saw the doctor twice, but he would only offer sympathy. For seven days and nights I didn't sleep—my body was a physical wreck but my mind was constantly active. I felt ready to explode, dogged by paranoia, having to lie on my bed and withdraw in silence. I needed to be alone, I wanted to talk to the Movie Maker, plead my case, beg for mercy, but how could I do that with two other guys there? They'd have thought I was mad. Anyway, they had enough to do fighting their own wars.

Sunday dinner time came. When the landing officer opened our cell door I told him I was withdrawing, but he just looked at me and said,

'You can do it, you've done it before.'

My mind was screaming 'No, I can't do it,' but finally I persuaded him to let me see the wing officer.

I walked into his office—what could I say? How could I explain the Movie Maker, paranoia, withdrawals? So I did a turnabout and just asked if I could be taken down the block—to the isolated punishment cells. At least there I could be alone. With tears running down my face I tried to explain that I felt sick, that I was breaking up inside.

To my surprise he immediately sent for the hospital staff and the welfare officer. I was amazed to find them so understanding—even sympathetic. In the end they put me in a single cell in the same wing where I could handle my withdrawal alone without upsetting anybody else. I was relieved: if anyone else saw me breaking up I would have lost yet another battle in the war. I would rather die than admit defeat, so for five more weeks I suffered in silence.

At the end of that time I was due to appear in court. I was glad to see Pat had recovered enough from her nervous breakdown to get there, but she looked defeated, frail and helpless. She couldn't come to terms with losing both me and Saffron yet again.

We got a surprise. For the first time ever the judge seemed to sense our helplessness, seemed to understand the battles we'd fought and nearly lost. To our amazement he sentenced me to twelve months imprisonment, suspended for two years. I walked free—but I knew I was still enslaved in the continual battle for survival and sanity.

First stop was to see the psychiatrist and renew my prescription, then home. We were horrified to find that the landlord had changed all the locks, and the remains of our furniture and personal belongings were strewn around his garage. Pat and I just shrugged. What the hell. We picked up Saffron's toys and belongings and walked away burdened with carrier bags. What else did we have to lose?

As usual in my anger and frustration, I turned to the only friend I had, who never let me down: the needle.

The elixir of destruction. Pat and I clung together in the darkness trying to console each other, haunted by thoughts of our lost children.

Now we were homeless, and that meant no chance of Saffron being removed from care. We saw her every day at the Social Services day centre, and spent our nights on the floor of a visiting room below the DRI psychiatric block. It wasn't that bad: at least we were first at the pharmacy for our prescriptions each morning.

After about six weeks, we found a single room in Doncaster, and the landlady said we could have Saffron in with us if she was allowed home. So when we were summoned to court again to plead our case for parenthood, we entered with grim determination to go down fighting. I might have bowed in shame and defeat to the Movie Maker, but I would never give up my fight for the right to be a father to my children.

The Doncaster court was full of people: prosecution solicitors, Social Services representatives, nurses and a whole lot more, all hell bent on retaining custody of Saffron. Pat and I weren't even allowed a solicitor unless we could pay him ourselves. What a joke. Another struggle we had to face alone.

The prosecution made an eloquent speech, laying down the law about why Saffron should remain in care; he called person after person to state from their vast professional knowledge why this was in Saffron's interests. Then I was allowed to speak. I asked only one question.

'Remember you're on oath today. Have you ever known Pat or me to mistreat our daughter in any way?' One by one they answered, 'No.'

When the magistrate summed up, he said he

appreciated our hardship due to the fact of our addiction, and appreciated the concern of the Social Services. But he felt it would be to Saffron's advantage to be returned to her parents on another three years' supervision order. The prosecution turned grey, the Social Services people seemed unable to move. As for Pat and me, someone had smiled on us again and bathed our lives in sunshine.

Although I had surrendered to my psychotic nature and paranoia, I wasn't defeated. All I had done was to allow the puppeteer the freedom of his strings. I'd stopped fighting and accepted what I had become.

Within a week of the court victory we answered an ad in the local paper, and moved into a house in Bentley, Doncaster. It was a strange set-up: an old lady living on her own, and as we moved in she moved out. We tried to rebuild our lives once again.

The summer of 1982 drifted along. Days were spent at the DRI where we felt secure, nights I spent at home listening to the Movie Maker analysing the day's events and planning the future. It was like being psychic: I listened to the voices in my head, then set out my day accordingly, armed with knowledge of his plans. I was always one step ahead. I had accepted this state as part of life, though I never admitted to being sick, so I retained the outward appearance of sanity.

Then suddenly out of the blue the old lady said she wanted her house back. Where would it ever end? I could see no future. Every time we were settled and seemed to be winning, another catastrophe reared its head. I resigned myself to losing Saffron for good. All the years of fighting real and imagined enemies was beginning to wear me down—I was just another candidate for the funny farm. Perhaps they'd let me and Pat share a room.

One evening about eleven there was a knock at the door. Oh no, we thought, we don't want to see anyone at this time of night. The knocking was persistent, so we called,

'Who's there?'

'Alex,' came the reply.

Oh no, I thought again. We'd known an addict called Alex some time ago—he was the last person we wanted to see.

Eventually I gave in to the persistent knocking and opened the door. To my surprise it wasn't that Alex at all. The young guy explained that he was at Bible college—Different, I thought—and that our psychiatrist had mentioned us to a friend of his who had passed on our address to him, and here he was.

Alex said he'd once been on drugs himself, but he'd found religion. That's all we need now, I thought. I wasn't very keen on listening, but the guy sat himself down in our tiny front room and began to talk. It seemed like the first time in my life that someone was talking to me, not at me, not about drugs but out of a desire to be friendly. The thing that struck me and Pat most about Alex was that he hadn't come to take, but to give.

He tentatively started sharing his testimony with us, about how he'd met this guy called Jesus and had been saved in prison. Strange, I thought. I sensed in Alex a person I could relate to—he'd fought his own wars and somehow won through. He gave us ten pounds, and asked if he could come back another day. Why not?

Three days later, Alex was the last person we expected to see: bailiffs, yes. Alex, no. Yet here he was again, this time bringing us a Bible. What's he after? I thought. Try as I might, I couldn't suss him out. Why was he prepared to give up his time to visit us? There must be a reason.

Alex's visits became more and more frequent, and Pat and I both began to look forward to them. Even the Bible reading he seemed to enforce on us was a kind of blessing in our continuous need. When Alex was in our home, the war seemed far away.

One evening we even found ourselves agreeing to his suggestion that we should go to church with him. So one Sunday evening, plucking up our courage (and armed with methadone and valium), Pat, Saffron and I set out. Walking into Bentley Pentecostal Church was a fearful experience for me: after all, the last time I'd been in a church I'd taken the Movie Maker in with me. Would God remember? I don't think he did—if he did, he never showed it.

The place wasn't what we expected. My memories of church as a child were of a dreary droning of religious words that meant nothing to me. Here we were greeted by handshakes, warm smiles and genuine friendliness. The hymns weren't what we expected either, people were singing, clapping and having a whale of a time. Different, I thought.

I don't remember what the preacher preached about, but I was impressed by his enthusiasm. The service finished with a song called 'Bind us together, Lord'. The people put their arms round each other, swaying to the music. Me, I was lost in the beauty of it all. I'd been touched by something other than the Movie Maker, and it felt good.

We began attending the church meetings: we wanted to have what those people had. Then one Sunday evening the preacher called out that there were people in the congregation who needed to meet with God. Suddenly Pat rose from her chair and headed for the front of the church. I couldn't believe my eyes, but I couldn't let her go alone. Plucking up my courage I joined her. The guy laid his hands on us and suddenly started shaking. His voice boomed out, filling the church with power and authority. I don't know what happened, but I looked at Pat and there seemed to be a glow about her; she seemed different, a Pat I'd never known before. As we left the church that night I was determined to know more about this guy called God and his son Jesus Christ, who could do all that to people.

By now Alex had set up a meeting with David Brown a director of this drug rehab called Abbots Leigh. At our interview David found out my real name: it was strange to be called Ron after all this time. Don I knew, Ron I didn't. Anyway, he said from now on I was to be called Ron. So be it. Why not?

Things began to move fast. David promised he would help us, and offered Pat and me a place at Abbots Leigh. Over the previous weeks I'd been reading my Bible, and found to my amazement that I could relate to this guy Jesus—if only for his suffering and concern for the lost.

We spent that last evening, 13th February 1983, getting completely stoned. We needed to be psyched up for the trip the next day. We'd said our farewells to the friends we'd made at church: now we prepared ourselves for the journey of a lifetime.

In two months our lives had been turned upside

down. Sixteen years had gone by, years of near insanity, total humiliation and frustration. The past we knew about, but the future seemed to lie in someone else's hands, someone else who would become very real in the years that lay ahead. There were many battles still to win: the war would go on for a little longer yet. But our fears were mingled with hope. We had a chance at last.

Psalm 31:9–18

Be merciful to me, O Lord, for I am in distress;
> my eyes grow weak with sorrow,
> my soul and my body with grief.
My life is consumed by anguish
> and my years by groaning;
my strength fails because of my affliction,
> and my bones grow weak.
Because of all my enemies,
> I am the utter contempt of my neighbours;
I am a dread to my friends—
> those who see me on the street flee from me.
I am forgotten by them as though I were dead;
> I have become like broken pottery.
For I hear the slander of many;
> there is terror on every side;
they conspire against me
> and plot to take my life.

But I trust in you, O Lord;
> I say, 'You are my God.'
My times are in your hands;
> deliver me from my enemies
> and from those who pursue me.
Let your face shine on your servant;
> save me in your unfailing love.
Let me not be put to shame, O Lord,
> for I have cried out to you;
but let the wicked be put to shame
> and lie silent in the grave.
Let their lying lips be silenced,
> for with pride and contempt
> they speak arrogantly against the righteous.

10
Abbots Leigh

The night had drawn around us like a big black cloak. It was scary, driving up the long bumpy track to Abbots Leigh: huge trees were caught in the beam of the car headlights, casting strange shadows, weird shapes that mingled with my hazy thoughts. Pat and I had become town people: we felt uneasy here, miles from anywhere, surrounded only by dark countryside.

There flashed through me a sudden urge to run, to run back to the understanding I knew, but the feeling passed as quickly as it had come. We drove into the courtyard of the house, and I was amazed to see how big it was. Abbots Leigh was a late-nineteenth-century country house. It had at one time been a huge estate, but the ravages of time had reduced it to a house and two small cottages with fifty acres of run-down land. How Abbots Leigh came to be in God's hands is someone else's story.

I can't remember who first greeted us, but they called David and his wife Jane, who came running into the hall. They put their arms around us both and made us welcome: Strange way to greet people, I thought. We'd hardly got our breath back when David told us we'd be staying in one of the cottages for a while, so we headed back into the darkness, carrier bags in hands. A girl called Rita showed us the way, and told us the cottage was the home of Rory and Susie, but they were away on holiday.

Their cottage seemed like heaven, with the homely touch of a log fire added. It had an air of calm and serenity, a stark contrast to the years of squalor and turmoil that lay behind us. Barry and his wife Linda, who lived next door, were waiting for us: Barry and Rita had been given the job of looking after us in the coming weeks.

As we sat talking with Barry and Rita that first night, Pat and I both felt muddled: confused, excited and afraid all at once. That morning we'd picked up our prescriptions of methadone at the DRI as usual, as we had done for years. Six hours later we were sitting in someone else's house talking to complete strangers about a new life. God. Jesus. It was too much for us to take, all in one day.

In bed that night we sat holding hands like two orphans snatched from the flames. Had we made the right decision? Drifting off to sleep took a long time, but as I dozed I was aware of a new feeling: the war was coming to an end. This was one place the Movie Maker couldn't intrude on. Here there would be no hidden eyes, no cameras. No, this was the place I'd been searching for, where I could come to terms with my past life; a place of renewal.

Next morning Barry woke us for breakfast. I knew what breakfast was, but I hadn't experienced it for what seemed like a lifetime—especially food. Our breakfast in the past had always been a fix in the toilets of the DRI. When we got downstairs it nearly blew my mind: the table was laid with coffee, cereal, eggs and bacon. Sitting down with Pat, Barry and Rita I felt completely out of place. We'd only ever sat down at a table like this in cafes—at home we had our meals on our laps in front of the TV. It was a completely new experience, something I'd long, long forgotten happened in the mornings. I realised that we weren't just going to get off drugs here. Our whole way of life was going to be turned upside down, and replaced right way up again.

Even more confusing was saying prayers before we ate. Holding hands around the table and asking God to bless our food and our day—it seemed childlike. What next? I thought as I tucked into my food. I found I was looking forward to our first day at Abbots Leigh.

Breakfast over, Pat and I decided to go for a walk. The scenery that greeted us completely blew our minds: the serenity of the countryside was mind-boggling after the noise and dirt of Doncaster. We stood hand in hand looking out over the rolling fields, the woods and hedgerows. I felt at peace. After Doncaster this felt like heaven. But we'd only been out for about ten minutes when we had to go back to the cottage—the old fears of the Movie Maker were gradually creeping back. Maybe all these people weren't in league with the Movie Maker, but surely they must be aware of his schemes? Could they come to terms with me? Could I come to terms with them? Only time would tell.

That morning we had a continual stream of visitors wishing us well. Most of them were residents in the house, and it was good to meet a guy from Doncaster called Mick. We didn't know him but apparently he knew us, or at least of us. Everybody was very concerned about withdrawals: they expected us to get sick the very next day. This worried me at first. Did they know anything at all about addicts? Addicts don't have genuine withdrawals so soon—they may scream and shout and work themselves up into a frenzy in psychological withdrawals, but not physical ones. Still, it felt good that they were concerned for us. That evening as we got ready for bed my mind seemed numb, unable to take in what was happening to us.

On the third day Barry took me over to the main house to occupy my mind doing a little painting. Pat was put to work peeling apples—no rest for the wicked. Although I wanted to contribute to the painting I was feeling very weak. My concentration seemed to be shot away: I couldn't even hold the paintbrush for more than ten minutes at a time. So Jimmy and I spent most of the day drinking tea and sharing our experiences—me, of my old life, him, of his new life now in Jesus. It all sounded completely alien to me, but I sensed that Jimmy was genuine and full of heart.

On the morning of the fourth day I was alone in the cottage, so I decided to play a music tape Rita had lent me. I was surprised to find it was a praise tape—should have known, really. The music was different, the words soothing. I sat in a chair, completely absorbed in the sound filling the room. It seemed to penetrate right into my war-torn body. It felt almost like being stoned, yet I felt no fear, no threat from the Movie Maker. I was completely oblivious to my surroundings, drifting off in a sea of serenity. Then one song touched something in me I'd long forgotten existed.

Jesus, name above all names
Beautiful Saviour, glorious Lord
Emmanuel, God is with us,
Blessed Redeemer, living Word.

When the song ended, I knew I had to listen to it again. Wind the tape back, turn up the volume. I sat back to listen. Something was stirring inside me as I listened to the words. When it finished I rewound again, fascinated by the sound. It was as if the angels themselves were singing the song just for me. My head was filled with the presence of peace.

There I was, completely alone, a hardened street fighter melting under the influence of a song. I played it again, and fell to my knees. It was like tripping out on LSD without the colours. Tears were running down my face. I felt embarrassed: what if someone came in and saw me? The more I played the song, the more the tears streamed from my eyes. In the midst of it all I found myself talking to God, perhaps to Jesus, I don't know. I started to say how sorry I was for the way I'd treated Pat, how sorry I was for all the things I'd done, the chaos I'd caused, all through the endless tears.

I got to my feet. This is silly, I thought, I'm a grown man. Yet I seemed hypnotised by the music and the words. I felt as if a great weight had been taken from my body. The anguish, the pain, the screwed-up emotions of all the years poured from my body like a flood, to be replaced by a peace I'd never known before.

I looked up through my tears and saw Pat and Rita standing in the doorway. Blow it, I thought, Why should I be ashamed? I wanted to tell Pat what had happened, how I felt, but my head was buzzing. So to save time I just put the tape on again and told her to listen. She knelt down with me—I don't know if she felt what I felt, but she was moved by the words.

I took hold of Pat and clung on to her as I cried. As I held her I felt something I'd never felt before, a love for Pat the person, not the person she had been but the person she would become. Outside the sun was shining, inside I was glowing. An hour later I was still bursting into tears. I felt like a little boy not lost but found. Something had happened inside me—what, I don't know. But I wanted to find out.

That night I talked to Barry about my experience. He listened patiently, but I noticed he kept smiling, more to himself than me. What did he know that I didn't? Barry picked up his Bible and turned to the book of Joel.

> I will repay you for the years the locusts have eaten—
> the great locust and the young locust,
> the other locusts and the locust swarm—
> my great army that I sent among you.
> You will have plenty to eat, until you are full,
> and you will praise the name of the Lord your God,
> who has worked wonders for you;
> never again will my people be shamed.
> Then you will know that I am in Israel,
> that I am the Lord your God,
> and that there is no other;
> never again will my people be shamed
> (Joel 2:25–27).

Barry explained to me that God wanted to restore all those spoiled and wasted years, years 'that the locusts have eaten'. What struck me most were the words in verse 26: 'Never again will my people be shamed'.

How those words filled me with hope. If there was one thing that bothered me it was coming to terms with the shame I felt from my past life. It felt good, listening to Barry talking about restoration, forgiveness, new life in Jesus Christ.

The past forgiven, then forgotten by God—that's what I wanted to hear. But coming to terms with that would be a different matter. Barry read on:

> And afterwards,
>   I will pour out my spirit on all people,
> Your sons and daughters will prophesy,
>   your old men will dream dreams,
>   your young men will see visions.
> Even on my servants, both men and women,
>   I will pour out my Spirit in those days
>
> (Joel 2:28,29).

He said that God would pour out his Spirit on all people. Had I experienced that already? I certainly felt different—my mind was more open to hear God's word. I couldn't understand yet all the bits Barry read out about prophecy, dreams and visions—that seemed too much like the old life. Still, I had come to Abbots Leigh finally to surrender. I looked forward to the day when I'd be able to understand God's word better.

For the first week at Abbots Leigh we didn't see much of the other people who lived there. What we experienced from those we did meet was a genuine love and concern, something completely alien to the world we'd come from.

On the Sunday morning the whole community gathered in one of the ground-floor rooms which was set aside for such meetings. I say meetings because they weren't church services as I understood them to be: nobody dressed up in their Sunday best. We went to the meetings because we wanted to be there: not out of compulsion, or a need for religion and all its tradition, but because we wanted to come together, people who were working through the problems of life together, getting to know Jesus the man on a more personal level.

That first Sunday Colin Urquhart took the meeting, as he was the leader of the Bethany Fellowship, to which Abbots Leigh belonged. I know now that the ministry at Abbots Leigh was very charismatic. I'd got used to that, a bit, in the Pentecostal Church in Bentley, Doncaster, but here in the small room I suddenly felt very out of place—all the people seemed so much at ease with each other. Yet through my fears and apprehensions I sensed that same love and affection I'd been getting from people all week. It calmed me, and I even began to enjoy 'praising the Lord' as they called it. Praising certainly seemed a great way of removing people's barriers: when the Spirit of God comes, his people become one.

Colin's sermon fascinated me. He talked about our lives before we'd become Christians, how they'd been cluttered up with sin and with circumstances beyond our control. The word sin was new to me—I had no real idea what it meant. I was soon going to learn.

Colin illustrated our lives by making a cup of tea. Different, I thought. He held up a plastic jug full of hot water, to show how our lives were at the beginning: man and woman were first created pure and sin-free, clear as water. Then he put some tea bags into the jug—by now I was engrossed. As he stirred the tea bags the water changed colour: sin. Separation from

God. Darkness. To me, sitting there in that crowded room, all this was great stuff, the explanations I'd needed to hear.

Colin poured out the tea he'd made, and pointed out that there was something needed to make it drinkable: milk. He added the milk and of course the tea changed colour—the effect of the Holy Spirit of God, he said, being poured into a life of darkness. Then he added sugar, saying God wanted to sweeten up our lives with the life of Jesus within us.

It was so simple, it was mind-boggling. But he hadn't finished yet: taking a spoon he stirred the tea vigorously, saying that every so often God needs to stir up his people, disturbing our lives for our own good. How true.

I don't remember much more—I'd taken in so much. But I came away that Sunday morning with an awful lot of questions answered by the simple act of making a cup of tea.

Rory and Susie were returning from their holiday, so it was decided that Pat and I would move into the main house. Seven days had gone by. Inside, my life was in turmoil, all my emotions were at sea, tossed to and fro on a continual tide of uncertainty. The old person I had been was being stripped away, to be replaced by a new person I knew nothing about.

And still the expected withdrawals had not emerged. In the past I'd suffered agonising times of torment: stomach cramps, hallucinations, aching limbs, cold sweats. This time was different: there was nothing. Pat and I were amazed at the lack of physical withdrawal symptoms—perhaps prayer really was powerful. I remembered that on our last night in our church at Bentley, the pastor had asked for people to take part in a prayer chain throughout the night for the next two weeks. All those people were thinking of us, caring for us, holding us. Later on, we found out that the people at Abbots Leigh had been constantly praying for us, too. How thankful we were for those prayers, offered by all those loving and sincere hearts.

God was beginning to move in our lives in the miraculous. But although the physical side of our addiction was being dealt with by prayer, the psychological side had somehow been forgotten. Perhaps all those caring, praying helpers just didn't understand enough about addicts. Sleep had become impossible for more than an hour or two at a time, and my head felt as if it was spinning, hazy and cluttered up with past and future. As I walked around the estate I seemed to be two feet above the ground. Something was happening inside me that I couldn't do anything about.

My past life could be summed up in the words of Proverbs:

> Your eyes will see strange sights
>   and your mind imagine confusing things.
> You will be like one sleeping on the high seas,
>   lying on top of the rigging.
> "They hit me," you will say, "but I'm not hurt!
>   They beat me, but I don't feel it!
> When will I wake up
>   so I can find another drink?" (or in my case, drug)
> (Proverbs 23:34,35)

It would have been so easy, then, to give up and run back to the security we thought we once knew. That verse in Proverbs is about alcoholics, but what goes on in the alcoholic's mind is no different from what goes on inside the drug addict. Although Pat and I knew very little about Jesus Christ, we did know the power that the old life had over us.

One day, David told us that we were new creations: the old had passed away to be replaced by a new life in Christ. He showed us a passage in Romans: Romans 6:1–14. Dead to sin—alive in Christ. I knew what David said made sense and was right. And it felt good. But to experience it, or believe it, was just too much for our minds to comprehend right then. The past was still too real, the new life too new.

The old life we could understand, but we had yet to experience this new life for ourselves. I knew from my past life that if you don't experience it, it isn't real. As we went to bed that night I prayed that Christ would become real to me. Not an emotional experience like the worship music that brought me to my knees in tears, but a tangible reality that I could live my new life in.

I read 2 Corinthians 5:11–17. Paul says 'Therefore, if anyone is in Christ, he is a new creation; the old has gone, the new has come!' (2 Cor 5:17). He could have just written 'If anyone...'. But he included that word, 'therefore'. It emphasises that you are—not 'maybe', or 'am I'. You are a new creation. Therefore the old must pass away to allow the new to come about. With words like these echoing in my mind, I set out accordingly to follow Christ with all the enthusiasm I'd had when I went out to score drugs in the old life: determined to win, no matter what the cost.

Physically we didn't feel like new creations: our bodies were wrecks, weak and disjointed. Sleep was becoming more and more of a problem to us, but we were determined not to see a doctor for a sleeping draught. We'd had lifetime of doctors. If Pat and I were going to beat this thing we would beat it together, with the help of God and our limited understanding of him. Why? Because we knew deep down that God was real and Christ was the only person who wouldn't let us down. I don't know how we'd come to know this in such a short time—it can only be explained by the lives of the people God had placed around us. It's hard to put into words. David and his wife Jane, Colin and his wife Glenys, John, Shirley, Barry, Linda and all the residents showed us a love and affection, a care and understanding we'd never known before. If this was what Christ had done for them, then we wanted to be like them. We had become children—no longer orphans, but children, welcomed into the family of God and Abbots Leigh.

Pat and I had moved into one of the bedrooms in the main house. We pulled the single beds together, and at night we'd lie there hour after hour, tossing and turning. Morning would arrive to find us completely exhausted. One evening David came to see us in our room, and the conversation quickly turned to the problem of sleep. I remember saying to David that sleep was a natural bodily function, a time of recuperation. Our bodies were screaming out for sleep yet our minds were working overtime—it seemed unnatural.

David seemed to have a brainstorm: he suddenly rose to his feet with a revelation that could only have come from God. He said that sleep was a gift of God himself. If that gift was denied us, there must be outside influences fighting against the natural function of the body. He went on to explain that there was a battle going on in the spiritual realm for the complete healing and salvation of our being, and that only the authority of Christ could overrule the demonic forces that were trying to snatch away the seed that God had planted in our lives. We agreed completely, because often we felt like giving up just because of the physical exhaustion that came through our lack of sleep. The only answer, David said, was prayer. Go for it, then, I thought. Anything for a good night's sleep.

David's prayer was another new experience for us. He started speaking in a strange language—the New Testament gift of tongues. I got used to it after a while—several people at Abbots Leigh used to pray like that. I used to call it shander-agandering, because that's what it sounded like to me. At the time Pat and I both thought he was throwing a wobbler. David laid hands on us and confronted the forces of Satan that were snatching our sleep away, and replaced them with the peace of Jesus.

We went out like a light and slept the whole night through without waking once. We'd witnessed yet again the power of prayer, the power to overcome the unnatural and replace it with the natural. Pat and I had learned yet another lesson about Christ the healer.

In our second week at Abbots Leigh Pat and I were working around the house and gardens—another new experience. We spent the afternoons resting, catching up on all our sleep lost in the previous weeks. Sometimes I worked in the fields with Vic, or fed the chickens and cared for the goats. The country air was doing me good. God had removed me from a hostile environment and placed me in the security of the countryside. I say security, because it would have been impossible for us to come off drugs the way we had, if we'd still been living in Doncaster. The place held too many memories. There were too many old acquaintances, too many places where we knew we could get drugs. Abbots Leigh was ideal, 250 miles from our old environment, a long way to go back whenever we felt like a fix. We needed protecting, even isolating, for our own good. We needed time out from the oppression of city and town life. We needed time to allow Christ to heal and restore us, time to get our heads together, away from the attractions of the world.

Two weeks after entering Abbots Leigh we were told we'd be moving to a bedsit in Haywards Heath. The news completely blew our minds away—we felt we weren't ready for this. David explained that they had no accommodation for married couples, and that we'd only be sleeping there: all the rest of the time we would spend at Abbots Leigh. In this Abbots Leigh was no different from the majority of drug rehabs in Great Britain: no place for the married couple. Still, we were here, and here we would stay, forever grateful for the God-given opportunity to remake our lives.

11

Renewal

Abbots Leigh wasn't a drug rehab as such: there was no organised work programme or structured rehabilitation. It was just a community of Christians living a community lifestyle. The three couples in the main house lived like extended families, and Pat and I moved into David and Jane's family. So although we no longer lived in the house itself, we still had all the benefits of having them as counsellors and friends.

Looking back, I can see it was a pretty amazing set-up: there were middle-class, working-class, punk rockers, lesbians and ex-addicts all living together under one roof, under the authority of Jesus Christ. What held it all together was the Holy Spirit—vibrant and powerful, always ministering hand in hand with Jesus, changing and transforming lives.

Pat and I were getting stronger by the day. I learned more about myself from David in three weeks than I had in sixteen years as a drug addict. During one of our counselling sessions David began to explain about the powers of darkness and light. He read out to me 2 Corinthians 4:4–6:

> The god of this age has blinded the minds of unbelievers, so that they cannot see the light of the gospel of the glory of Christ, who is the image of God. For we do not preach ourselves, but Jesus Christ as Lord, and ourselves as servants for Jesus' sake. For God, who said, "Let light shine out of darkness," made his light shine in our hearts to give us the light of the knowledge of the glory of God in the face of Christ.

The god of this age—Satan, paranoia, the Movie Maker, drugs—had blinded us to the light of Christ. As we listened to David it all seemed to make sense. The Movie Maker was revealed at last. I knew about Satan: for years Aleister Crowley (the beast, as he was affectionately known to his friends) had been one of my heroes. His book, *The Confessions of Aleister Crowley*, had been one of my favourites. In the darkness that surrounded my past life I had constantly sought and often communicated with the demonic. Once David heard this he began to pray with me, bringing me to repentance and forgiveness.

I have realised since then that for any young Christian repentance must be the centre of conversion. Without repentance there can't be any true conversion or moving on with God. Some young Christians today come to repentance through either simple emotion or shallow words, and they grow up as crippled Christians. Seeds sown in shallow soil can be plucked out of the ground by the birds of the air; seeds sown in the heart of repentance will eventually produce an abundant harvest.

Listening to David filled me with the desire to know Jesus better. God had taken hold of our lives and poured out his Spirit on us. The years of havoc under the rule of the Movie Maker were being erased from our minds, to be replaced by the love of Christ. 'For it is God who works in you to will and to act according to his good purpose' (Phil 2:13). It was evident to me that God had indeed begun to work in us. Now it was up to me and Pat to do our bit. We believed; now we were ready to be renewed, with all that would entail.

God's work of renewal starts on the inside at conversion and gradually works its way outward. Through his son Jesus Christ, God had begun to renew my mind, an essential step if I was to come to completeness in Jesus Christ. I saw why when David showed me Romans 12:1,2.

> Offer your bodies as living sacrifices, holy and pleasing to God—this is your spiritual act of worship. Do not conform any longer to the pattern of this world, but be transformed by the renewing of your mind. Then you will be able to test and approve what God's will is—his good, pleasing and perfect will.

I wanted to do God's will. 'Submit yourselves, then, to God. Resist the devil, and he will flee from you' (Jas 4:7). The enemy has no right to our minds, and I could play my part in resisting by being open to God's word.

David began showing me the scriptures that would help God's work.

> For though we live in the world, we do not wage war as the world does. The weapons we fight with are not the weapons of the world. On the contrary, they have divine power to demolish strongholds.

> We demolish arguments and every pretension that
> sets itself up against the knowledge of God, and we
> take captive every thought to make it obedient to
> Christ (2 Cor 10:3–5).

Take captive every thought? Easier said than done, I thought. The mind is a complex piece of machinery: it takes time to mend, time to readjust to new thought patterns, new teachings. Thirty-five years of continual bombardment from the world doesn't evaporate overnight.

It takes willpower to say no to drug addiction. The key lay in asking God to give me that willpower, then being determined to fight for my salvation, and not being put off when I felt like giving up. A woman doesn't have a baby unless she's prepared to teach it to walk. The same applies to the word of God. He doesn't tell us to be born again unless he's prepared to teach us how to walk in his way—thank God for that.

Another lesson I had to learn was to confess my weaknesses to God. When I was a child, if I fell down I ran to my parents for help. Now I learned to lean on some of the people God had placed around me. I read Romans 7:7–25, a passage all about struggling with sin, and I was reassured that God understands what we're going through. It helped to be assured of my salvation: 'Who shall separate us from the love of Christ?' (Rom 8:35) and to understand the kind of battle that was really going on inside, and to be assured of the outcome from Romans 8:38,39:

> I am convinced...that neither angels nor demons,
> neither the present nor the future, nor any powers,
> neither height nor depth, nor anything else in all

creation, will be able to separate us from the love of God that is in Christ Jesus our Lord.

As I began to discover God's word, many answers to the past seemed to fall into place. The mind has always been Satan's prime target for attack, and when I read 2 Corinthians 11:3 I was amazed to see how Paul had feared for the early church in Corinth, that their minds might be led astray: 'But I am afraid that just as Eve was deceived by the serpent's cunning, your minds may somehow be led astray from your sincere and pure devotion to Christ.' How real those words are, for although God had begun to heal me in many areas, my mind was still fighting to take everything in, and I didn't find it easy.

I asked David how I could combat the old fears and thoughts that continually flooded my mind, and he led me to the scriptures again: Luke 4:1–12. It's the story of Jesus' temptation in the wilderness, and there I found the answer to Satan. When he was tempted by the devil, Jesus resisted him with the word of God—back to James 4:7 again, 'Resist the devil and he will flee from you.'

My most persistent problem was paranoia—something common to all addicts. I now believe that drug-related paranoia is induced by Satan, and that it can be healed in the name of Jesus. How? By deliverance, counselling and constant prayer. In the past Satan had used my innermost fears to hold me ransom, and one of his chief weapons was my deep guilt, which undermined my self-confidence and hampered my natural, God-given abilities. I had always felt inadequate and useless.

Now I knew that if I was to see a victory over my

paranoia I had to take hold of the word of God and somehow find a way to believe it. Over the next few weeks I talked to the other residents at Abbots Leigh about my paranoia, and they were always helpful, often giving me relevant passages to read from my Bible.

> No temptation has seized you except what is common to man. And God is faithful; he will not let you be tempted beyond what you can bear. But when you are tempted, he will also provide a way out so that you can stand up under it (1 Cor 10:13).

It was a help to realise that God knew what was going on in my mind and was able to provide answers and an escape. I found another useful piece of advice in Colossians 3:1–4. 'Since, then, you have been raised with Christ, set your hearts on things above, where Christ is seated at the right hand of God' (Col 3:1). The more I discovered God's word, the more I opened up my mind to him, and so allowed the Holy Spirit to minister healing through the authority of Christ. I understood at last that Satan is, after all, a defeated enemy.

I was learning so much, so fast, that my mind was often in a muddle. But I sensed that now I'd begun to grasp many answers that I'd been searching for for many years.

When God begins to move in our lives, he doesn't stop unless we become a stumbling-block. So it seems right to spend a little time on the scriptures that helped me through the early stages of recovery. I thought of these as the keys to victory.

As we came to the cross in repentance Pat and I had

asked God to forgive us for all the things we had done, for all the people we'd unknowingly set on a road to destruction by supplying them with drugs. We had to put on the armour of God, and to learn what that meant for us in our lives.

> Stand firm then, with the belt of truth buckled round your waist, with the breastplate of righteousness in place, and with your feet fitted with the readiness that comes from the gospel of peace. In addition to all this, take up the shield of faith, with which you can extinguish all the flaming arrows of the evil one. Take the helmet of salvation and the sword of the Spirit, which is the word of God (Eph 6:14–17).

The belt of truth, we decided, meant being truthful and not holding out against God and repentance. We accepted that God was in control of our lives, governing what happened in our minds and bodies as we slowly began to come to terms with our new life.

The breastplate of righteousness, for us, meant being aware of the light of Christ living in our new life. We had to try hard to combat old habits, and bad language was a good place to start. After all, 'the things that come out of the mouth come from the heart' (Matt 15:18).

The gospel of peace told us that the battle has already been won on the cross of Calvary—try believing it. When anger and resentment flooded back, we asked Christ to replace it with his peace, and grant us his forgiveness.

The shield of faith protected us: we had to believe

that day by day we were being changed, and not give Satan a foothold by doubting.

A further protection was the helmet of salvation. We had to go on believing that we were saved, even if on some days we didn't feel like it or even act like it. A helmet protects the head and mind, and the confession of Christ as Lord of our lives closed our minds to the temptation of the old ways.

The sword of the Spirit taught us to fight the enemy with the word of God, teaching and correcting our lives every day. We submitted to the working of the Holy Spirit in us.

Finally, one of the most important lessons we learned was that Satan never takes a holiday! We had to stay alert and watchful, wearing the armour of God and ready for the battle against old habits, old temptations.

God's work of renewal takes time. Pat and I were fortunate because we had each other to lean on when times got hard. We were really determined to get off drugs, and we were prepared to go through anything to do it; nevertheless there were many times when I felt that I was just being brainwashed and wanted to give it all up. Yet there comes a time in all our lives when we have to stop running from God: like Adam and Eve in the Garden of Eden, we now had no place to hide.

The teaching we were getting from David helped us to understand what was happening to our lives inside, but coming to terms with it was still often very hard and painful. There seemed to be so much to learn—we thought we'd never make it.

That's when God's grace became evident to us. For years I had searched my mind for my real father, allowing my imagination to run riot, living in dreams and hopes that he would be rich and powerful. Suddenly I found I didn't care any more: through Jesus I had found the Father of all. The knowledge of God's love fulfilled all the yearnings of those years of searching. God had become my Father and I had become his child. Being illegitimate didn't matter any more.

12

Learning to Live Again

Three months went by: we settled into a routine, coming to Abbots Leigh each day and going back to our bedsit every night at about ten. Pat and I grew stronger day by day, and my paranoia was rapidly subsiding. At last my life seemed to be getting on an even keel. And now we were going to be reunited with Saffron—Alex and his wife were driving her down. We were so excited at the prospect of seeing her again, and it would be good to renew our friendship with Alex. Saffron was going to live for a while with David and Jane—that had been decided with the agreement of the Social Services Department.

At last the great day came: as Saffron got out of the car she looked uncertain, afraid. Would this be just another time that Mummy and Daddy would come into her young life only to disappear again? We spent the next two months coming to terms with parenthood, and our responsibility for the care of our daughter. This was quite easy for me, as I didn't have any real responsibilities at all—David and Jane had taken them over. But it was harder for Pat. Yet again someone else was dictating how she should bring up her

108

daughter, and she was often in conflict with Jane and David. However, these conflicts were quickly resolved or pushed underground, as we found we had so much to learn about family life. We'd always believed we'd got it together in the past, but now we realised that we had to start again from scratch.

The fact that Pat and I had been drug addicts meant that Saffron had been brought up in a pretty unnatural environment. Her life had been one of constant hospital visits, with parents who were continually under the influence of drugs. It was going to be as hard for her as it was for us to come to terms with this new life. Saffron was shy and insecure: she'd witnessed too much at too young an age. There had been no continuity in her life as she'd had to endure the incredible highs and lows of our addiction.

Now we all needed security—the sort you get from a stable home environment. What we needed now was a permanent home, with constant help and advice available. A place where we could all grow together in the knowledge of our new-found faith in Christ. I could see that one way to bring about this stability was for me to find a job. Because of the unusual situation of having a whole family to minister to, David was placed under enormous pressure to find us a home, since at that time we couldn't live at Abbots Leigh. Eventually he found us a house in nearby Handcross, where many of the Bethany Fellowship had made their homes. It seemed at the time the most logical place, as we would be surrounded by other Christians. David also found me a job with a guy called John, a builder who was part of the Bethany. Everything seemed to be falling into place.

Looking back, I can see that we'd fallen into the

universal trap of recovering addicts. Physically we were feeling good—much inner healing had taken place—and because we felt good we thought we'd made it. We still had our fears for the future, but these were overshadowed by our desire to be reunited as a family.

I hadn't worked in sixteen years, so to get a job was a big step for me. Still, I felt confident and able. John was an amazing guy—he knew all about my past life, yet he was still willing to give me a chance and employ me. At last the skill of bricklaying I learned in prison would come in useful. Not only did John give a job to me, he also gave one to a young guy called Peter. Peter had come to Abbots Leigh because he was addicted to gambling: he spent all his money and lost his flat, and ended up sleeping rough. Here we were, the two of us, given a new chance in life. God had been good to us.

At Handcross we started out with great expectations and lots of enthusiasm. Pat and I were constantly reading our Bibles and trying hard to put into practice what we learned. While I was out working, Pat spent her days with Rita, running the house and looking after Saffron. It was in Handcross that God first began to speak to me about working in the future with addicts. My reaction wasn't good. Leave it out, Lord. Who, me? You must be kidding! This was another new experience—actually hearing God's voice. The trouble was, I hadn't learned to distinguish God's voice from Satan's, so I let it ride. The future could take care of itself: there was so much to do in the present.

For the first few weeks everything seemed to be going well. I was enjoying my new work and felt at peace. Then when I got home one day I sensed that something was wrong with Pat. She'd begun to resent Rita being with her every day.

'After all,' she said, 'what does Rita know about home and family? She's never even been married.' Rita's role was to help Pat around the house during the day time, and be a friend if needed. That night Pat and I sat down and talked. I was surprised to find I was married to someone I knew very little about. Pat seemed a complete stranger. In the past our lives had evolved from one tragedy to another: I'd married Pat on drugs, and now she was drug free I was meeting a new person in Jesus Christ.

Being in Handcross isolated us. Although there were many good Christian people around us, we didn't have much in common with them. They didn't understand our old life, and we didn't understand theirs. They came from a different world. The only thing we seemed to have in common was Jesus, but even their conceptions of him seemed different from ours.

Another problem was money—not the lack of it, but having too much. At the end of every week I would find myself with £140 in my pocket, money I didn't even know how to spend. In the past we'd spent every penny we had on drugs or food. Coping with this new-found wealth was the beginning of yet another long and painful experience.

We still had contact with Abbots Leigh on Sundays and one evening each week. But beyond this we had to come to terms with life on our own. We still loved the Lord and wanted desperately to move on, yet we couldn't escape the feeling that we'd been deserted, left on our own to fend for ourselves. I suppose if anyone was to blame, I was the chief culprit. I still had this 'no surrender' attitude. I hadn't yet fully learned to submit, and because of this my family would pay the price in the months ahead. Our relationship was gradually turning sour: we had constant rows, each putting the blame on the other. The new life was fast disappearing back into the old one.

During our stay in Handcross, David had bought an old cinema in Brighton, planning to convert it into a coffee shop and the headquarters of the new street evangelism work which God had called him to. David had told Pat and me that he would like us both to move to Brighton and work in the coffee bar.

The thought of Brighton filled us both with fear: I spent long nights wrestling with God about this decision. It was during this time—often one of blind panic—that God began to speak to me very clearly, warning me of impending disaster for us as a family if we were to go to Brighton. God had told me we must go to Abbots Leigh as he wanted to disciple us.

My life was filled with confusion yet again. Was it God speaking? Or had the Movie Maker returned? I was beginning to get paranoid again. I still hadn't learned to discern God's voice. As a young Christian I was totally in conflict with God and man.

One evening I went to Abbots Leigh to attend a meeting for those who'd supposedly been called to the work in Brighton. I took Barry aside and told him that I was attending the wrong meetings, that I should be in the group working at Abbots Leigh. Barry was concerned, and made an appointment for me with Colin Skeates, who was now the director of Abbots Leigh.

Soon afterwards, Colin came to see me in Handcross. But I didn't have the courage to tell him how I felt, or how clearly God had spoken to me about

LEARNING TO LIVE AGAIN   113

Abbots Leigh. With Colin I felt just as if I was in the headmaster's study: all my feelings of inferiority came flooding back. Somehow I found myself telling him that everything was fine, that both Pat and I were doing great.

For weeks I struggled inside, getting more and more confused and uncertain of the future. By now I had become a prime target for Satan, and it wasn't long before he raised his ugly head. One evening one of the residents called with some cannabis. We were too weak to resist and say no. The old life was back with a vengeance, leaving our new life to slip slowly away.

I still wasn't happy about the move to Brighton, so I had a talk with Michael Barling, an elder of the Bethany Fellowship. This time I told all. I told him what God had said about going to Abbots Leigh, and about discipleship for a lasting structure for our family and home. Michael passed it all on to David, but it didn't help. According to David, God still wanted us in Brighton. Part of me was sure he was wrong, but who was I to judge? He'd taught me so much, and done so much for me. So I did what he told me, even though, deep down, I felt it wasn't what God wanted for us.

Seven months had gone by since we first came to Abbots Leigh. And here we were smoking dope, calling ourselves Christians, and worst of all, heading into a hostile environment once again: Brighton.

While we were living in Handcross, Mick, the guy from Doncaster, had married Ann, a girl from Abbots Leigh. They moved to a flat in Brighton, but the rent was too high, so Pat, Saffron and I took it over from them. I'd struggled against moving, but we still had to trust that God was in control, even in our sinful state. The flat was leased by Rescue City (the new work in

Brighton) so I began to negotiate with the landlady to take over the lease. I was still working and we thought we could just afford it. So perhaps everything wasn't as bad as I thought.

Over the past months I'd begun to look to David to supply all our needs—I hadn't contributed anything to our upkeep, even though I was earning a good wage. It was the same with the new flat: somehow I expected David to go on producing whatever we needed. This was a fatal error. I was looking to man and not God to supply my needs. And the more I relied on David, the more I blamed him for the way things were turning out.

Mick became a regular visitor, and it wasn't long before we were both going out to local pubs, and smoking dope constantly. The rot had set in. I still believed in God, but I found I was completely unable to stop the gradual slide back to my old way of life. Looking back, I know why I isolated myself from the family of Christ: I was ashamed of my backsliding, but I didn't have the will to stop it.

One evening I came home to find Alex moving us out of the flat. We'd been aware that the lease was up, but we'd pushed aside the urgency of it—thinking, I suppose, that Rescue City would live up to its name and come to the rescue. Alex moved us out with pain in his heart, and Pat and I watched bewildered as our belongings were loaded into his car. The move was over as suddenly as it had begun: Pat, Saffron and I stood in the street with nowhere to go, so once again Alex agreed to take Saffron home with him. Pat and I would have to fend for ourselves. If this is Christianity, I thought, you can stuff it.

The slide back to our old life was now complete.

LEARNING TO LIVE AGAIN 115

That night Pat and I stayed in a bed and breakfast place, totally confused, angry and frustrated. Was this just another ploy of the Movie Maker? Was he playing another card in the game of life? It seemed to us that the light of Christ, that had come into our lives so miraculously, had been snuffed out by one act of man.

The following day we all moved into a hotel for the unemployed. One room, three beds, and a breakfast of scrambled eggs every morning. Me, I was so angry I jacked in my job and turned my back on everything that God had done for us.

Pat and I have often looked back at that situation and can now praise God for it. Because I was slipping back into the old ways our marriage was in danger of collapsing. If we'd stayed in the flat, I think we'd have ended up in the divorce court. There were going to be many more times in our lives when we wouldn't understand God's plan for us, times when I would cry out to God in anger and frustration, asking him what he was doing. Why me, Lord?

But all things work together for good for those that love him. When he placed us in that sea-front hotel, with addicts, prostitutes, alcoholics and such, God reminded us of what he had done for us, by showing us our old ways through the people now around us. However, at the time I never felt God was still in control of our lives.

Living in one room brought me and Pat close together as a family unit: because of our situation we had to rely on each other more. Lots of times I wanted to give up and go back to Doncaster, but to what? I would have gone, though, if it hadn't been for Pat and Saffron encouraging and praying for me all the time. During our stay in the hotel I had no contact with

David or with Rescue City, though Pat and Saffron often went to the coffee bar. Me, I was too proud, too ashamed at my backsliding, to be able to face the people who had cared for us so much.

Living in the hotel in Brighton stripped me once more of my responsibilities to my family, against my will. Again I felt inadequate as a man. Often I would stay in bed to try to hide from the world, hoping that when I woke up everything would be all right again—it never was. It was one of these days when Alex called to see us. At first I wouldn't speak to him—I felt angry and ashamed, and there was a barrier between us. But Alex is a persistent guy, not easily moved by stubborn pigheaded people, and he insisted that we all go to a 'Moving on with Jesus' meeting at Worth Abbey. In the end I agreed to go.

'Moving on with Jesus' meetings were held each month by the Bethany Fellowship. I knew that David and all the other leaders of Rescue City would be there, and I thought it would be a good opportunity to give David a piece of my mind. I didn't think much about the meeting with Jesus part.

When we arrived, Worth Abbey was filled with about 500 people. I felt lost and ill at ease, tied in knots inside by all my sins. I didn't listen too much to the speaker—my mind was on other things—but at the end of the evening there was an altar call. I knew in my heart that I needed to respond, but my pride wouldn't let me. Fortunately Pat intervened, and taking my hand she virtually dragged me to the front for prayer.

As I walked to the front of the abbey I had this awful feeling of all eyes being on me. Deep down I knew that I had to meet afresh with Christ and ask forgiveness for the way I'd turned my back on all he'd done for me.

Also, I needed to be reconciled to David. When we prayed together I found myself confessing my sins of backsliding; simple prayers from the heart. I fell on my knees to the Lord to beg forgiveness, and somewhere during that prayer time I knew that God had forgiven me. Now I had to learn to forgive myself and face up to my responsibilities.

On my way back to my seat I saw David, and I plucked up my courage and went over and arranged to meet him for a chat. David welcomed me back with open arms, asking me to forgive him for not coming to see us at the hotel. My relationship with David wasn't what it had been before, but time would heal that.

A week later we moved out of the hotel into a bed and breakfast place nearer the coffee bar. It was still only one room, but it was cleaner and nicer than the other one. Coming to terms with Christ and my pride allowed God to continue his work of healing in our lives. God had showed me and Pat how it used to be in our old life—and when we saw that, we could see more clearly what he'd already done, and what we'd already achieved. And if we were willing, God would do immeasurably more.

If I look back and ask what lasting lessons did we learn through all this, I'd have to say this. We had to look to God, not man, to supply our needs. And we had to be prepared to submit to those God had placed over us to teach and correct us.

13

Learning to Trust

The lesson we learned in those bedsits and hotels in Brighton was a powerful one. We'd been expecting David to do everything for us—provide a home, provide a job. We thought all we had to do was sit back and let it happen. Now God was beginning to teach us to trust him for our needs.

When we came off drugs our lives were put through a washing machine: Christ washed them clean, and now God was beginning to do the ironing. Ironing out all the creases in our lives would be a life-long experience, changing us on a day-to-day basis. Why? So that we may one day be presented to the Father, whole and worthy to be called true sons and daughters of God, to take our place with Jesus before the throne of our Father in heaven.

We knew that one day we would be with the Father—however, this confession of faith did very little for us in our present situation. We needed to grow in God's ways for those words to become a reality. We had to experience that personal relationship with Christ in our everyday living, and somehow come to terms with the past and use it towards the future plans God had for us.

Another move was in store for us, this time out of our one-room bedside into a flat. The flat was an answer to prayer, a place where Pat and Saffron could begin to settle at last, where Pat could begin to build a home. Home life was an essential part of our walk with Christ, as we began to put into practice everything God had been teaching us through his word. If we were going to walk in God's ways, first we had to learn to express our Christianity inside our home. It's no good being Christians in the world, preaching love and God's salvation, if you're still living your old life at home. How could we minister to addicts in the future if we couldn't come to terms with our new lives ourselves?

God's order for Christian living is that God is sovereign over all: first God, then family, thirdly ministry. Why? Because God is head of the Christian family; only then is Jesus able to minister his healing and restoration—which was what we needed to grow and mature in our faith. I found that I had to be obedient to God, because the security of the Christian family comes when the man is in complete submission to the Father. If the man is at war with God, eventually he'll be at war with his family and lose his God-given peace. When the man comes under the authority of God, the woman has security and peace of mind, because she knows her husband is doing the will of God.

Family structure often breaks down when the woman takes on the man's role—it makes him feel inadequate as a man. In our modern society, many families break up because of unemployment. Work is a gift from God, and through providing for his family man reaches his full potential as the provider, a role which is inbuilt in his nature. When this is removed, the man often becomes disheartened and unfulfilled. When he can fulfil this role, he has a better chance of keeping his family intact.

Another problem is that many Christians seek a ministry first, often pushing aside family and friends. If the ministry fails, they become disillusioned with their faith and turn their backs on God. Any ministry can only blossom when the family home is secure. By getting our priorities right, we can grow into maturity first, and then move on into whatever ministry God may call us into. I believe that the key to Christian growth lies in our home lives—not in the number of meetings we attend. Get this right, and God can use us anywhere.

When we moved into the Brighton flat it was the first time we'd really had a chance to get to know each other. We could give Saffron the security of a home, and allow her to grow and experience family life. Saffron was four years old, and in her short life she'd been moved around eleven times. She'd become the centre of our lives, yet in many ways we'd stifled her growth by clinging on to her out of fear of losing her. The flat enabled us to do the things most parents take for granted: walks in the park, games of football, going to the beach.

For me, family life was a new experience, and at first I found it hard. I often pushed my responsibilities of fatherhood on to Pat, who at the time seemed far better equipped to handle them. There was so much to learn, so much to experience together as parents, that our past lives had withheld from us.

One of our major problems was lack of money. We

LEARNING TO TRUST   121

were no different from any other family living on Social Security, striving to make ends meet. Our frustration at not being able to give Saffron the things we'd like to often led to loud rows. Throughout this trying period I was unemployed, and often times seemed hard. Still, we never went without like we had in the past, and somehow we managed to survive. Without God in our lives I believe we'd have gone under many times. We still sympathise with people living on Social Security: life should be more than just making ends meet, with no hope or future, living on dreams that it'll all be different tomorrow.

What kept us going was the hope we found in Christ and a grim determination to fight for our new life. We drew strength from God's word and the daily evidence that our lives were changing. 'Seek first his kingdom and his righteousness, and all these things will be given to you as well' (Matt 6:33). In our seeking God had answered: he would provide our daily needs, but not necessarily our wants.

By now I was going every day to the old cinema which was being converted and renamed the City. I was still unemployed, but I filled my time painting, and talking to the down and outs of Brighton who came looking for help. It was there that Pat and I found we had a great love and concern for the addicts and alcoholics who visited the coffee bar. God's discipleship had begun.

I noticed how much our lives were changing through Saffron: she became more settled and confident as we grew together as a family under God's caring hands. Our lives became more and more stable week by week, and God began to heal more wounds from our past.

One of my great regrets was not going to see my mother. I kept putting it off until finally it was too late—she died of a heart attack, leaving me feeling guilty at not visiting her and trying to patch up the past. I wish I'd said sorry for all the torment and worry I brought into her life through my drug addiction. I hadn't seen my family for years, so Pat and I went to the funeral in Caerphilly, South Wales. I was apprehensive about seeing my Dad and sisters, but I knew it was something I needed to do.

My brother and sisters were all married now—I hadn't seen Ann, my oldest sister, in twenty years. It was strange, arriving at my father's home: I felt like a total stranger. The first person I bumped into was my brother, and I didn't even recognise him, though Pat did: she said he looked like me.

My Mum was cremated. The funeral service was very short, and I felt helpless as I watched the coffin vanish into the depths of the crematorium. So much had happened in the past, and now any reconciliation would have to be done by me alone, in the quietness of my soul. After the funeral we went back to Dad's house to talk. My family couldn't understand when I told them about our new lives in Jesus Christ. But before we left, Dad took me aside and said he was glad for us all, that at last we'd started to sort our lives out, and he wished us well for the future.

On the way back my mind was filled with 'if onlys'. My mum went to her grave not knowing if her son was alive or dead. Though we'd never got on all that well, I knew deep down that she'd loved me very much.

My mother's funeral taught me yet another lesson: the importance of reconciliation within the family. All my years of suffering as an addict had affected my parents. They'd had to fight their own battles, answer their own questions, and come to terms with life, with their son's addiction hanging over them like a shadow. How they coped with it can only be told by the countless parents who go through similar experiences of helplessness, feelings of inadequacy, and the many heart-piercing moments, drowned in memories of what might have been. They are torn and tormented by their love for their children, who are trapped in a situation beyond their parental control.

Life goes on. As we grew as a family we were able to give more of ourselves to others. Sundays in the City outreach centre found us providing meals for the many lost and homeless of Brighton. Rescue City coffee bar opened its doors on Sunday mornings and became a place of worship for people who had no church to go to, or who felt that a traditional church didn't offer them anything. After the service they were given a hot meal.

Sundays became the highlight of our week. Pat and I felt at home with the lost and lonely people who were going through experiences we'd been through in the past—people we could relate to. On Sundays thirty or forty men and women came in through the doors, maybe just for a meal or a listening ear. This gave David an opportunity to preach the gospel of Jesus Christ. On Sunday nights we opened up the coffee bar to offer times of healing and prayer. Lots of people only came for a meal ticket to start with, but ended up giving their lives to the Lord. God had begun his work for the poor and needy of Brighton—not just in a spiritual way, but in a very practical way as well.

For us, God had begun his discipleship of our lives. Through Rescue City Pat and I became involved in the work of God. There were many opportunities to pray with people and share our experience of Christ, giving our testimony of how God saved us from utter destruction on drugs, and was now showing us a new way to live our lives, drug free. Pat often invited some of the guys round to our flat for tea. As we gave more of ourselves, we started to experience God's love for the lost: God was beginning to reveal his heart to us.

One evening I asked David if I could start going up to Abbots Leigh on the work bus. It ran daily, taking people from the streets into the serenity of the countryside, providing care and love and practical work. David seemed pleased that I wanted to go each day, and said that he felt it was the right thing for me at this stage of my Christian growth. At the time I didn't realise the significance of my return to Abbots Leigh—I'd put out of my mind the words God had spoken to me all those months ago. By now Pat and I had got used to the idea of allowing God to shape our lives. If he wanted us at Abbots Leigh for further discipling it would be at a time of his choosing, not of ours.

Travelling from Brighton to Abbots Leigh every day gave me a sense of purpose and achievement. I was still unemployed and receiving state benefit, but working there on the farm and grounds was yet another step towards full recovery.

I'd been working there for about a month when I was summoned to see Colin in his office. Looking back, I suppose it was a sort of interview—Colin wanted to know where I was at. But at that time, to be honest, I didn't really know where I was at. I was just grateful to be given an opportunity to start again.

Interviews are never easy, and I hadn't ever learned

how to handle them. The whole situation was totally alien to me, because of my past life. I'd isolated myself from the real world, and for years I'd moved only in the world created by my addiction. Everyone I'd known in the past took drugs. People like Colin were alien to me: they might as well have come from a different planet. The only people I'd ever known with any authority were judges, probation officers, social workers, or psychiatrists: people who were constantly taking either my freedom or my children away from me. So I felt ill at ease as I entered his office.

Colin and his wife Glenys were not the typical, run-of-the-mill directors I'd imagined. I sensed in them a genuine concern for me and my family, yet I was still totally unable to communicate with them. Colin asked how I was—and up came the barriers.

'Fine,' I replied.

He talked about the future, but all he got from me were vague answers. I wanted to tell him everything God had been saying to me, but I felt embarrassed. Why? I just didn't trust authority. He had to prove himself to me before I could open up to him. And I needed time to build up relationships, because in my addiction I'd locked away my innermost secrets and desires for so long. The past was still too real, the future too uncertain. I left his office frustrated because I didn't yet have the ability to trust my fellow men: once again I felt defeated. I longed so much to unburden myself, but fear of rejection kept me silent.

From my limited experience of God I knew that he has the ability to heal instantly. A surgeon can remove the cause of an illness on the operating table, but when the patient recovers, the scars are still visible. The reality of the healing doesn't penetrate the brain until the bandages have been removed and the scars have healed. My family and I had been healed in many ways, but the bandages hadn't yet been removed or the scars healed. Me, I knew that at some stage I was going to have to place my trust in someone. I'd started to do it with David, but circumstances had placed more barriers between us. I also knew that God wanted us at Abbots Leigh, and so Colin and Glenys must be the people he had placed over us. They were the ones I had to learn to trust.

My inability to communicate my feelings had become a stumbling-block to God's complete healing. God knew it—I knew it. But changing my attitude was a different matter. As I went home to Brighton that night there was a war going on inside me. God was at work stirring me up. Tea time with Pat and Saffron was a stormy affair: I kept snapping at Saffron for no reason at all. In the end I decided to take a bath— perhaps it would relax me and calm me down.

As I sat in the bath I heard God speaking very clearly to me.

'Ron, I want you to go back to Colin tomorrow and have another interview. Only this time I want you to tell him all I've said to you concerning your future. Ron, you need to start trusting. Without trust you are an ineffective Christian. If you want to work for me with addicts you need to be able to communicate with people, like Colin. Communication is what my church is founded on. The ability to relate my word is what it's all about.'

I felt devastated at hearing God speak to me like that. I felt as if I'd just been told off—probably had.

Full of enthusiasm, I jumped out of the bath and rushed to tell Pat. She was over the moon, yet she stayed so calm—it was as if she already knew. Now I witnessed another aspect of Pat I'd never seen before: her calmness. God showed me a new, reassuring side to her nature, and I loved her ability to accept what I told her without question. That night Pat and I talked as we'd never talked before. As I confided in Pat, God showed me that I did have the ability to open up to other people without fear of condemnation.

For a couple of weeks I'd been painting indoors at Abbots Leigh, and the next morning Colin popped his head round the door to say Hi'. I knew this was my opportunity to speak to him again, so I blurted out the words,

'Colin, God's told me to talk to you about that conversation we had yesterday.'

Colin looked utterly bewildered. He invited me into his office, and once again as I went in I felt like a little boy. I sat down, feeling the sweat running down my arms: my palms felt sticky and my stomach was knotted up with fear. But Colin really did have the knack of making people feel at ease. After to-ing and fro-ing for a little while, he said,

'Ron, why don't you just come out with it and tell me what God's been speaking to you about?'

For the next fifteen minutes I waffled on all about how God had spoken to me, starting in Handcross and ending up the night before in Brighton.

'Fine, Ron,' Colin replied. 'God's been speaking to me, too, about you and your family. I'd like you to look for a house in Haywards Heath, so you can become more involved in the work here at Abbots Leigh.'

Confirmation was the last thing I really expected, but it was a huge relief. At last I was beginning to be able to tell the difference between God's word and Satan's. Two months later we moved into a rented house near the centre of Haywards Heath. God was beginning to bring about everything he'd told me about all those months ago. At Abbots Leigh our discipleship would begin in earnest.

14

By Water and Spirit

Saffron was beginning to settle into her new school, Pat to work around the house, and I was doing house maintenance. Life seemed good. Pat and I still had our differences, but now we could resolve them without the violent outbursts of the past. Colin, Glenys, Barry and his wife Linda were all people we could turn to in times of trial, to share what was happening in our lives. God was teaching us to trust him and also the people he'd placed around us. It still wasn't easy, but as time passed we built up relationships founded on our love for Christ and each other.

My days spent with the guys who came up on the work bus from Brighton gave me even more insight into God's love for the lost. Every morning we all met together as a community for praise and worship, giving thanks for the day and everything God had done for us. Often these meetings developed into personal revival meetings—we found ourselves confessing our weaknesses to each other, and then praying for the lost.

There is great healing in this open confession within a community of believers. The word of God wasn't thought, it was spoken at Creation. What goes on inside us must eventually be spoken out if we're going to receive God's complete healing. Not that we can't communicate with God through our minds, but the act of speaking out allows the Holy Spirit to flow through our being. It wasn't easy for Pat and me to confess our sins out loud to others, but as our relationships blossomed we began to open up more and more.

Together we read the first two chapters of the first letter of John, all about walking in the light, confessing our sins, and loving our brothers. It taught us to speak out from the heart and not let things, situations or people turn our hearts hard. We realised how important it is not to harbour ill feeling and let it fester away inside us, snatching away our peace.

Lots of times I couldn't understand what was happening within the ministry at Abbots Leigh. Sometimes I would rub against Colin and his leadership team, and those times left me feeling frustrated and irritated. Often I disregarded what I'd learned from the scriptures, and bottled up my feelings until I was at war with God and everyone else. This feeling of opposition to God affected my daily living, and I soon realised that unless I dealt with such situations quickly, they would fester inside me for days.

Learning to surrender was hard work for me, completely opposed to my past life. My pride was still a major stumbling block. I believe God gave me the ability to bounce back, and many times I've had to swallow my pride and go to people I feel angry with and ask their forgiveness (even when, sometimes, I still felt I was in the right). In the confession of our sins together we grew in the knowledge of our Lord Jesus Christ—and it was never as painful as sticking a needle in my arm. It was all part of growing and maturing in Christ.

The ironing process of God's discipleship is often painful, as any woman knows if she lets the washing get too dry: the ironing becomes hard work, and it's often impossible unless she dampens it again. God's steam iron is his Holy Spirit, what God uses to get the stubborn creases out of our souls. At conversion I received God's Spirit, but I hadn't yet seen it materialise in my life through the gifts of the Spirit (1 Cor 12:1–11).

There still seemed to be something blocking the flow of God's Spirit through me. Then one day it suddenly dawned on Pat that we hadn't ever been baptised in water—so how could we understand the baptism of the Spirit? Before Jesus was fully equipped for his ministry he was baptised in water, and then God also filled him with the Holy Spirit to empower him for the future. Today I believe that many young Christians go through crippling experiences because their church leaders fail to baptise them until they prove themselves worthy. How can they, if their conversion is incomplete?

In Acts 2 on the day of Pentecost we find Peter addressing the crowd. When they ask, 'What shall we do?', Peter answers them, 'Repent and be baptised' (Acts 2:37,38). Those who accepted the message were baptised—not twelve months later, but right there on the spot. I believe that they, like Jesus, were baptised in the Spirit on their conversion. This baptism is vital to equip us to cope with the emotional imbalance that often occurs at our birth into a new life—a life filled with challenges and a whole new way of thinking.

Baptism in water was important to me, too, because

it would enable me to express my inner assurance of the love of Christ in an outward act. And baptism in the Holy Spirit, by the laying on of hands, would help me to understand God's ways more, and bring revelation to his word. This was going to be my next step along the road to understanding. I'd come so far, yet everything still seemed so painful at times. Why? I was sure it was because I hadn't received the revelation of the Holy Spirit. There were certain areas of teaching I still couldn't understand because of my past experience with the Movie Maker.

I've met many people who claim to be born-again Christians who fail to show any evidence of the spirit-filled life—even the least of the gifts, tongues. Speaking in tongues is a sign of a spirit-filled Christian: the apostles asked for no other evidence from the believers.

I'd heard God's word, spoken to God, loved him, and had a personal relationship with Jesus. Yet I showed no outward signs of being spirit-filled. If God was going to use me, then I had to be able to make use of his gifts. If I was going to mature in Christ, then I needed to go through the same process that he did: baptism, both physical and spiritual. After all, Jesus' disciples spent three long years walking and talking with him, and in the end they still didn't really understand what he was, until the Day of Pentecost. So how could I?

Over the previous months I'd been faced with trials and temptations, and I'd lacked the power to overcome them. Now it was time to seek out the Holy Spirit. So Pat and I were both baptised in the swimming pool at Abbots Leigh.

When they asked me to give a testimony afterwards, I was gripped by fear—I didn't know what to say. Eventually I found myself confessing how hard I found it to say sorry to Pat. I admitted that I could be wrong sometimes, that I'd been hard in the past—sometimes near impossible. I asked God right there and then to give me the ability to apologise. I believe that I received from God what I asked for, and it was a great relief to see this gift coming to life in the following weeks. I still found it hard to do, sometimes, but it was so beneficial to our growth.

Two weeks later, during one of our community worship times, I had the opportunity to ask God to fill me with his Holy Spirit (Acts 19:1–7). I asked David to lay hands on me so that I could receive God's gift. He looked very surprised—his expression seemed to say, 'I should have done this a long time ago.'

David placed his hands on my head and asked God to fan into flame the spark of the Holy Spirit that had been dwelling in me from the first confession of my faith. There was nothing miraculous about it, but I sensed that now my conversion was complete. I felt better equipped to walk in the new way with Christ. David also had a word from God for me: 'When much is given, much is expected.' This made me think very hard about my responsibilities as a Christian. Through the baptism of water and Spirit my Christianity had now become a reality.

By now the work of Abbots Leigh and Brighton was maturing fast. In Brighton, many people were coming to know Christ as their personal Saviour, led by David and his team. On the practical side they were often helped to find accommodation and work. Those who showed a genuine committment to Christ eventually moved into Abbots Leigh on a residential basis to receive teaching and ministry.

It was during this period that Colin decided to run training weeks for people who felt called by God to minister to the poor and needy—those who, through no fault of their own, found themselves addicted to drugs or alcohol. The training weeks would allow people to learn about ministry, and also to give of themselves in practical ways, such as working around the house and gardens alongside the residents. Leading by example in a work situation is often the quickest way to build up relationships: it offers so many opportunities to put into practice the teachings of Christ.

The training weeks proved quite successful. For some people who believed they'd been called to this ministry, the experience was an eye-opener. Many arrived with stubborn, fixed ideas about what God wanted them to do, only to find out in a short time that for them, the cost was too great. But others would receive confirmation from God, and direction for their lives.

One of the keys to ministering to the lost can be found in Ezekiel 2:1–7. The Israelites there are described as a rebellious nation, to whom Ezekiel has to go and prophesy: 'The people to whom I am sending you are obstinate and stubborn...you must speak my words to them, whether they listen or fail to listen, for they are rebellious' (Ezek 2:4,7). Addicts are often stubborn people, showing the unbroken spirit of the world within them.

In my short time as a Christian I've seen many people fall by the wayside because of the pressures of this ministry. If you are called by God to this work, you must have total commitment. There is a spirit of rebellion in the young people of our nation today, rebellion against God and all he stands for. If we're going to win the lost for Christ, then first we must put our own house in order. So during the training weeks many who came found that first of all God dealt with them as individuals. God first appoints, then he anoints, then he sends out.

For me the training weeks were times of great learning. By now I'd decided to spend my God-given time there using Abbots Leigh as a mini Bible college: a place to learn and to be a witness to God in action. Sometimes I found it difficult, mixing with what I would call the middle class, and I was often critical of their motives. It was great that they were committed to dedicating their lives to working with addicts and alcoholics, but I was appalled at their lack of knowledge of the people they would eventually be ministering to. Good intentions and a kind heart just aren't enough.

How can anyone talk to someone who's paranoid, with drug-induced schizophrenia, if they don't have the first idea what's going on inside that person, or what they're going through? You can't take a person further than you've gone yourself. If you don't know what you're dealing with, you won't be effective—you may leave major problems untouched. Fear of the unknown, and fear of our own inability to cope with what we might uncover, both hamper our counselling. If you can't minister thoroughly, you'd better not do it at all: half-ministered people make half-converted Christians, unable to cope with either world.

The keys to ministering to the lost must be, firstly, to make sure of your calling. Be filled with the Holy Spirit, that unables you to minister in the gifts of the Spirit, and makes you willing to dedicate your lives to

God's work. Next, make sure that your prayer life has priority, because when you don't know the answers, God does.

Gain as much experience as you can before going into the ministry. Use the people God has placed around you: God gives us all individual gifts that often complement each other. And never be afraid to admit your mistakes.

The Christian world today is filled with would-be evangelists—many people feel there's a certain amount of glamour in that. The ministry to addicts doesn't look so attractive: it's a ministry of hard work, personal growth, and many heartaches along the way. It's a ministry of long working hours, often on shoestring budgets, causing great frustration. But the benefits are tremendous when you see with your own eyes God working through his Son Jesus, restoring and changing those whom the world had written off. It's a work worthy of its calling to those who minister under the authority of Jesus Christ.

With such teachings and personal observations I grew as a Christian. I had arrived now at the crossroads. To go on meant that I had to place my trust in Colin, with his God-given abilities and his vision of raising the likes of me—an ex-addict—to a standard fitting for Christ, to a place where I'd be able to stand on my own feet and see God's purpose for my life unfold. By now Pat and I shared a burning ambition to work with addicts, but we had to learn to walk before we could run.

The more we walked in God's way, the more the old life began to disappear. God taught us more by enabling us to be more involved in the training weeks, initially by praying for those he sent to us. It was a new experience, to pray for people we'd never met. It also gave us a chance to use the gifts of the Spirit, especially words of knowledge. Sometimes God would give us words for people who were coming on a course, and those words were often fulfilled during their time with us.

Pat and I had been working at Abbots Leigh for about six months when it was decided that we should move into the house. We were fully aware that working in a community was one thing; living in was another. It meant total commitment of a different kind: the sharing of our lives under the scrutiny of others. After long prayerful conversations with God, we decided that it was right. However, we didn't realise the amount of time we'd actually have to spend working. Community living was a full-time job: often on duty sixteen hours a day, open twenty-four hours to be on call.

This took its toll of our family life: I found myself giving more of my time to the guys than I did to my family. The work of God was beginning to place my relationship with Pat and Saffron on a precipice. I had to have many long hard talks with Colin and Glenys before I realised what was happening. Switching off was—and still is—a big problem for me as an ex-addict: I was used to living a life of constant involvement in the circumstances of addiction. Shutting off the mind takes will power.

As so often in the past, I had to learn that readjusting takes time and prayer. It wasn't the amount of time I spent talking to people that would solve their problems, it was what was achieved during that time. Addicts are notorious talkers and will spend valuable time in endless prattle. I needed to learn to shut up and not be drawn into long fruitless conversations, when I could be spending that precious time with my family.

It wasn't easy, sharing our lives, but God gave us the grace to come to terms with it, grow in it, and even begin to feel comfortable in it. Community life isn't for everyone, but if you're called to it it's an essential part of God's ministry—the ministry of family to people who have never experienced it before. After all, if God expected the guys to belong to the family of Christ (that is, the church) then they first needed to experience a family of Christians in reality. Community living was another one of God's lessons we learned through the sharing of our lives.

Another part of our maturing took place one evening during a training week. After three days of teaching, Colin lost his voice. He felt that God wanted to use our team—the one Pat and I belonged to—to do the ministering. When we met in Colin's office that day I suddenly sensed the presence of the Holy Spirit: during prayer time I felt a tingle running from my neck down through my body. I should have realised then that something unusual was going to happen. When Colin told me he wanted me to pray with people that evening, I was terrified. He went on to say that we could minister the Holy Spirit into peoples' lives; that we could be used by God to anoint and bring to life the gifts they would need when they began their own ministries.

As I walked from the office I found myself saying, 'Who, me, Lord? You must be kidding!' During the week Colin had been teaching from 1 Corinthians 1:26–29:

> Brothers, think of what you were when you were called. Not many of you were wise by human standards; not many were influential; not many were of noble birth. But God chose the foolish things of the world to shame the wise; God chose the weak things of the world to shame the strong. He chose the lowly things of this world and the despised things—and the things that are not—to nullify the things that are, so that no one may boast before him.

Now was the time to see if it really worked.

Our meeting started as usual with a time of praise and worship. Me, I couldn't really enter into it. I was still nervous and wanted the worship to go on all night. The nearer the time came to prayers, the more I began to shake inside. Finally the moment came, and Colin called us out to the front: me; Maggie, a punk rocker; Julia; and Susie on the guitar. Standing at the front I felt very conspicuous and out of place. I hadn't got a clue what was expected of me. Looking back, I suppose the training week people were as nervous as we were. Colin asked them to come forward when they felt it right, and for an awful moment I thought that nobody was going to ask for prayer.

God was merciful: the first person to come forward was Alan. He was part of the team, a guy from Doncaster who used to live with my old friend Jamie. Alan had lost one of his hands from injecting diconal, and for a terrifying moment I thought he was going to ask me to pray for the healing of his hand. To my relief he asked me to lay hands on him and pray that God would fill him afresh with the Holy Spirit. I laid my hands on Alan, and felt a surge of energy running through my body. Suddenly I was speaking out in tongues, asking God to release his Spirit.

What happened next took me completely by surprise. Alan suddenly shot across the room and landed on the couch. I thought, Blimey, what've I done? I'd done nothing. But God had moved in power and authority. Next came Gary, another resident. The same thing happened again, and this time Gary's head hit the wall. It was all too much for me, and I went over to see if he was all right. He was. I sensed that the air had somehow become electrified. The Holy Spirit had manifested himself—something I'd never seen before and probably won't again.

One guy came forward to receive the gift of tongues. By now the Holy Spirit had completely taken over, and I was no longer in control, if indeed I ever had been. The guy burst into tears, then into tongues, and then went out like a light at my feet. I looked across at Julia and Maggie as they prayed with people, and realised that they also were experiencing the power of the Holy Spirit for the first time: the evidence was the pile of bodies at their feet. Everyone who came forward and asked for the Spirit was granted their prayer.

I don't know how long we prayed with people like that—time seemed to stand still. I remember we sang 'Seek ye first the kingdom of God'. Then I knew that I was witnessing the Holy Spirit, alive and active. The room seemed draped in an orange-gold glow: I could hear the sound of a wind rising and falling, which seemed to rush round the room disturbing nothing. My first reaction was that I must be having a flashback on LSD. The music seemed to get louder and louder around the room, the orange-gold glow seemed to be jumping and flickering. The floor was littered with the bodies of those we'd been praying for. Then all at once the wind died down, the orange and gold faded as swiftly as it had come. I was completely exhausted.

Colin stepped in and began to bring our meeting to a close. The room was bathed in silence as we gathered on our knees to pay tribute to God. Even the silence seemed electrifying. Joining hands, we sang 'Bind us together, Lord'.

We met in Colin's room afterwards to give glory to God, but I felt devastated. Had I been privileged to watch another Pentecost, the moving of God's Spirit among his people? I needed to be alone, so I headed for our bedroom. No sooner had I sat down than I was gripped with fear. What had I done? What a fool I had made of myself. I would never be able to face those people again. Satan came in like a roaring lion to try to snatch away what God had shown me.

The next morning I slipped quietly into the back of the final meeting and sat at the back of the room, trying to hide my feeling of guilt at having such fears and doubts. I wasn't sure I could cope with it all. But God had shown us the immense power of his Holy Spirit, and his ability to anoint and equip his saints for the battles ahead.

15

Into the Future

'If anyone would come after me, he must deny himself and take up his cross and follow me. For whoever wants to save his life will lose it, but whoever loses his life for me will find it' (Matt 16:24,25).

The taking up of the cross of Jesus is our inner expression to the Father of our acceptance of Jesus into our lives. The following of Jesus is the hard part, the outward expression in our daily living. That's when we have to look at what we've already achieved, weigh up the cost, and decide whether or not to go on. When we turned to Jesus we died to the old life; when we followed Jesus we found a new one. One of my favourite songs used to be 'Stairway to Heaven' by Led Zeppelin. Now Pat and I were beginning to see that that stairway can be a long and frustrating climb.

The work at Abbots Leigh was continuing to flourish under God's hand, but the City, though growing, seemed to come under increasing pressure (mainly financial). It often seemed as though this ministry to the lost had been divided, not just physically, but also spiritually. For me and Pat, young Christians filled with a desire to do God's work, these were trying

INTO THE FUTURE 143

times. We even heard through the grapevine that a group of Satanists were actively praying against the work in Brighton and Abbots Leigh.

Quite often I retired to the tennis court (my favourite retreat) to wag a finger at God—I couldn't understand his purpose. But both Pat and I sensed that things were beginning to go wrong. It was as if the leadership was getting swallowed up in a sea of need—there were so many young lives now seeking help. I often took out my frustrations on Colin, and each time our conversations ended up in what I suppose you could call controlled misunderstanding.

One of the most evident signs that things were not as they should be was that my old and trusted friend Barry was leaving. It took me a long time to come to terms with this, as Barry and his wife Linda were an integral part of the Abbots Leigh leadership. Then Alex and his family went back to Doncaster. They'd all been good friends, placed around us by God, friends we could always rely on in times of need. Yet even amid these uncertainties God was still at work. People were still being saved, and placed on the road to restoration, and new couples were arriving to join David's team.

I'd started doing some basic Bible teaching once a week with the guys—a project that terrified me. Once again I had to find out that I couldn't do anything on my own: it had to be God working through me, enabling me to minister his word under the anointing of the Holy Spirit. We had good times together exploring the word of God—usually I learned as much as the guys I was teaching.

Then, in the autumn of 1985, Pat had a word from the Lord which she felt compelled to share with Colin and Glenys: Haggai 1:1–11. It's the passage where Haggai speaks for the Lord to the leaders of the nation, telling them that it's time to build God's house, and to stop being preoccupied with their own concerns. 'Is it a time for you yourselves to be living in your panelled houses, while this house remains a ruin?...Give careful thought to your ways. You have planted much, but have harvested little' (Hag 1:4–6). This powerful word devastated us, yet it seemed prophetic to our situation in the ministry. We'd thrown our hearts into the work, yet we'd achieved very little. God began to withhold his finances. In desperation, the ministry at the City began to look elsewhere for money; when even this failed, the leaders were left frustrated and confused.

Even now when I read that scripture I fail to grasp its full meaning. But we realised that the 'panelled house' had to be Abbots Leigh, and so Pat and I decided to move out. God had done so much for us, and under Colin's guidance we'd matured in our Christian lives. Now God was telling us to go out into the world, perhaps to see if we could survive beyond the protective confines of Abbots Leigh and the close fellowship of believers.

Colin and Glenys moved to Brighton, which made us feel very isolated. Then David resigned from the leadership. With David leaving, the vision for Rescue City faded. Colin took over from him, but we knew he was leader of a dying ministry. Our last community meeting was held in Hollingbury Gospel Hall, when we worshipped God together and heard David resign officially. As we gathered in that one room—forty people who had shared their lives together—I was filled with quiet sadness: it was like witnessing the breakup of a family. My eyes were misty with tears. I could see no future, yet I felt at peace with God. Throughout the meeting I was asking one question: why?

Perhaps God spoke to all of us that evening; at any rate, I know he spoke to me quite clearly. Pat and I had learned a powerful lesson some time before, when we'd put our trust in man and not God. In the work of Rescue City a similar problem had arisen: people had become dependent on David, and David's own obsession with the work had isolated him from the people God had placed in his care. Too many people were too dependent on Rescue City, and lacked their own vision. Their loyalty to David was stifling their own development, and preventing them from reaching their full potential in Christ. Of course there were many other factors contributing to the collapse of Rescue City, but that's not my story to tell.

The end of any work which God has inspired is often traumatic for the people involved. Why do ministries suddenly fold up? There are many reasons. But I believe that God takes us as individuals along the road to heaven. When we veer off that road, things begin to go wrong. Perhaps we'd tried to do too much, too quickly. Often God-given visions fail when we try to extend the work beyond what God calls us to.

Walking into the City building for the last time was another sad experience. The lights in the auditorium were off, except for the one shining on the huge cross hanging on the stage wall. For a brief moment I felt angry about our present situation. My mind was filled with 'if onlys'. Pat and I had been privileged to witness the power of God to change lives, yet here I was, standing in the shadows of the auditorium, seeing God closing doors instead. Sad though I felt, I knew

God was moving us on, to build on the new foundation he'd laid in our lives.

I went into Colin's office—the poor guy looked shell-shocked and tired. By now I felt at ease with Colin, and we'd built up a friendship over the last few months. I needed to speak to him, for I was aware of a great burden of fear and frustration. I wanted assurances from him that when the doors finally closed, all the people who had given their time and energy to the work, and who in some ways had become dependent on Rescue City, wouldn't be left as spiritual orphans. The City had become a church for both the full-time and the part-time staff. I felt it was Colin's responsibility to help them to move on into other fellowships.

Colin has always had a pastor's heart, and he quickly assured me that he would give help and advice to anyone who needed it.

'In the end, Ron,' he said, 'our walk with Christ can only go on if we do the walking. Spiritual crutches can do no good for anyone in the long run.'

Words of sanity, I thought. Reassured that Colin and Glenys would be available to anyone who called on them, I said my farewells to the City for the last time, and prepared for the move into Brighton.

When God decides to move, he moves quickly. He doesn't prolong an inevitable decline, but takes hold of situations and restores certainty. What had appeared outwardly to be a flourishing ministry had in fact been crumbling inwardly for a long time. Now the past was past. God is a God of new beginnings—new beginnings that would test my faith and my ability to provide for my family in both practical and spiritual ways.

With the help of Rory and Susie, Pat and I moved into

a flat in Brighton that we couldn't really afford—yet with God's help and provision from friends our daily needs were met. One of the Abbots Leigh residents, Steve, moved in with us.

It was essential that we find a place to worship, so with Colin, Glenys, and others from Rescue City, we eventually arrived at a fellowship called 'Abundant Life'. Fitting into our new surroundings was hard, and I found it difficult to adapt. I suppose I was still suffering from a sort of spiritual hangover: in truth, no matter what church I attended I never seemed to be satisfied. The inevitable happened and we left—a bad mistake at the time, because we didn't have another church to go to. In this way we entered into a period of spiritual limbo, one foot in the kingdom of God, and one foot in the world: seeds sown for trouble if not remedied quickly.

We stayed in our flat in Brighton for six months, and it became a place where ex-residents could come and talk, and often grumble about the past. Many of those who came were still filled with bitterness about the closure of Rescue City. Pat and I often found our loyalties torn: on one hand we could sympathise with those who felt hurt and let down, but on the other we knew the necessity of putting the past behind us. It's a sure recipe for disaster when hurting Christians get their heads together and try to justify their grumblings about present situations. Satan has a field day. If we allow the past to dictate the future, there can be no future. It would have been so easy then to fall into the trap many recovering addicts fall into—one foot in the past, one in the future, and no one does anything about the present. I'd spent too much time thinking like this: I knew I needed to deal with 'now'. Quickly.

What kept us going throughout this period was our desire to follow Jesus and eventually to work with addicts. With this implanted firmly in my mind, I went out to try and find work. Six months later we moved into a flat in Kemptown, but Steve went back to drugs, taking his destiny in his own hands. God had given him the right to choose. 'But as for me and my household, we will serve the Lord' (Josh 24:15). God was gracious and stepped in, providing me with a job as a painter.

I say God stepped in, because I believe my job was an answer to prayer. My prayer life at that time centred around finding work, not just for me, but for some of the guys who'd been through Rescue City and Abbots Leigh. I had no real skills as a painter, but I found myself starting up a painting gang, and taking on a contract to paint a block of flats. The work enabled me to provide for my family and also allow God to do some healing of hurts; it was a time of fellowship, although we struggled with our lack of professional skill. We made a living, through the grace of God, and learned a lot about our own abilities.

By now I'd completely written off the church and all it stood for, and once again I'd become a spiritual orphan—struggling in my faith while my Bible gathered dust upon the shelf. I hadn't lost my ability to communicate with God, and my desire to work with addicts was as strong as ever, but I still had feelings of frustration. Deep down, I knew that God had spoken to me about this, yet who was I? An ex-addict struggling to survive as a Christian alone—not by choice. The churches around me seemed to have very little to offer.

Those may seem like harsh words, but in fact they

were true. I needed to belong now, not prove my worth by attending church meetings for the next five years. I didn't want to join a club: I wanted to experience God through the Body of Christ. My biggest stumbling block seemed to be my past. Trying to come to terms with middle-class theology drove me even further from the church: after all, Jesus was a carpenter. If he'd been born in modern times, he'd probably have worked on a building site. Jesus was a man of the people, not a stone image in a building. Christ the Saviour, the forgiver of sins, the healer and restorer—it was knowing him that kept me going. Not sleepy Sunday morning services.

Often we held our own communion service in the front room, Pat, Saffron and me. We would sing, Saffron would bring us the bread and wine, and I would read from the word. We had great times together, allowing God to minister to us when all around us seemed to be crumbling. God was still the centre of our lives and our family, and our future lay in his hands only. The Bethany Fellowship, Abbots Leigh and Rescue City lay behind us. Through their teaching we'd been grounded in the word of God, and what we'd been through would equip us for the future.

During this period we'd had very little contact with Colin and Glenys, so we were surprised to get an invitation to a farewell party. They were moving to Bristol to work with Life for the World, a long-established ministry to drug addicts. My first reaction was 'Great!', followed by a feeling of sadness, for yet another cherished friendship seemed to be slipping away. We never attended their farewell party—I'd said enough goodbyes to last me a lifetime. My one prayer was that God would use them fully in his work.

With Colin and Glenys gone, the final chapter of Rescue City ended. We were sad to lose our friends, but were content in the knowledge that they were continuing to bring new life, through the Lord Jesus Christ, to people who'd travelled the same paths as us.

We were blessed in another way as well. Pat's son Steven was now eighteen and able to leave the home he'd been placed in by the Social Services Department: he decided to come and live with us for a while. His sister Lyn was now living with Pat's father. Life had turned a complete circle. I was amazed at how Steven accepted the past and all that had happened; he was overjoyed to see that his Mum had, in his words, sorted her life out. It was hard for me, trying to play father to a grown man, but Steven and I soon built up a friendship. Now he was living with us Pat and I had many opportunities to share the gospel of Jesus Christ with him, and he listened tentatively.

With the reconciliation of Steven and Lyn, another chapter in our lives was complete. In the following months I wiped the dust from my Bible and gave thanks to God for all his mercies. I put aside my thoughts of a future ministry to drug addicts, and concentrated on learning my new role as father and provider.

On New Year's Eve, 1986, Pat, Saffron and I took communion together, seeking God and praying for the young people of Brighton. That night I could get no rest, and God spoke to me again about working with addicts. Finally in desperation I prayed with Pat and asked God to give me a sign—I needed to know, for my own peace of mind. It didn't matter when it would come about, but I wanted an answer now, either way. If we hadn't been called to work with addicts, then I needed to know so that I could get it out of my system once and for all, and get on with whatever else God had in store for me. Having dared to ask God for immediate answers, I went off to bed and wrestled with my thoughts, and finally fell asleep in the early hours of the morning, tired out.

Later that morning I was woken by the phone ringing—it was Colin. Colin and Glenys were the last people on my mind, as I hadn't heard from them since they left Brighton for Bristol. Colin wanted to know if I was still interested in working with addicts. Was I hearing right? Yes. Apparently there was a vacancy in Bristol for a trainee staff member, and he could send me the application form. He couldn't guarantee me anything, but if God wanted me there, then that's where I should be.

I felt stunned as I put down the phone and repeated the conversation to Pat. Once again we'd witnessed the power of prayer. We'd poured out our hearts to the Father the night before, and again the Father had come up with the goods. With the restoration of our family now complete, God was ready to release us into the work of his kingdom. I had no doubt now of our calling, and no doubt that God wanted to continue his work in our lives. Life for the World was to be only a starting-point, a springboard into the future.

Pat and I spent three years at Life for the World, deepening our maturity and growing in discipleship. God led us to a church—the New Life Centre—where we were received with warm affection, and fed with the spiritual food that would sustain us in our work. The pastor, the Revd Jim Dick, helped and guided us as we worked alongside Colin and his staff, learning how best to help others and share the good news of Jesus.

When we made the move to Bristol, God showed me a scripture: Numbers 13:1–33. Moses sent out spies to explore the Promised Land, and many came back fearful; Caleb and Joshua recognised the dangers, but they trusted God, and their faith brought them to the Promised Land. During the years in Bristol my life has often seemed like a 'look and see' mission: looking at the needs of those caught in Satan's bondage of addiction, and seeing what rehabilitation has to offer. By faith we trusted that God would lead us through difficulties into the work he planned for us.

It has, in fact, been a difficult and rewarding time. As we've lived and worked with the addicts Pat and I have become increasingly aware that the drug problem is a greater menace than ever before. We see the moral values of society being eroded before our eyes, and aimless young people being caught in the trap of addiction. The only hope is Jesus—and if we as Christians are to fight the enemy, we must unite and work together.

Every time we meet we hold the very words of life in our hands: the word of God in the Bible. It tells us that God is so concerned for the lost that he sent his only Son into the world, and everyone who believes in him shall be saved. Salvation can come to the lost only when God's people respond to his call, and God is calling today: the harvest fields are ripe. This is the season of salvation. Who will go into the world and rescue the lost for Christ? I pray that God will raise up many more from his flock, to hear his call.

Pat and I have been privileged to do this work. It's a joy to bring the light of Christ into the lives of young people who are engulfed in Satan's darkness, and to begin to set them free from the chains of drug addiction. There is no greater calling to the church of Christ than to preach the gospel of Jesus in the dark world that surrounds us.

As we continued in this work—truly offering 'life for the world'—we found ourselves developing and changing. God's healing continued in our lives. As we moved from Abbots Leigh to Brighton and then to Bristol, we were aware that each community, with its Christians, its leaders and its pastors, was teaching us something new about our own walk with God in this world.

We are ready, now, to leave the sheltered communities which have nurtured us. The world no longer seems to us like a land of giants ready to devour us, but a land of opportunities to reach the addicts for Christ. Sure in the knowledge of our own salvation we can preach and teach the glories of the gospel. God has clearly told us to go out and take his light into the darkness. For if God is going to show his compassion to the addict, it must flow out of his church under the anointing of his Holy Spirit.

In the eyes of the world there seems to be no solution to the problem of drugs, but we who know God know different. There is one hope, one light, one life in Jesus Christ. Our task as the church, as the people of God, is to share the light we have.

Too often in the past men and women have come out of the church into work among addicts— sometimes labelled as 'para-Christian organisations'. They do magnificent work in the rehabilitation field, but they are isolated from the church. They don't get the support, either material or spiritual, they need and deserve.

As we look at the future of this work, we believe God is now saying that the addicts must be discipled within the church. Not in isolation, in little communities where they can accept one another, where there may be too few mature Christians to offer guidance. Instead they should be welcomed by the Church, drawn into the framework of existing youth work, into the worshipping life of the local fellowship. There can be no better starting place for the addict who truly wants to see his life transformed, than to be accepted into the Body of Christ.

We believe that God is saying to his church of whatever denomination, that it is time to work together, to join forces to combat the growing drug menace among young people. After three years in Bristol, Pat and I felt it was right for us to move on, into the next phase of God's plan for us. We left the secure community environment to go out into the world, into a new job, into local churches, to share and to teach from our experience.

Our long-term vision is to establish a discipleship/rehabilitation centre for addicts that will also serve the church, where Christians can come and learn from the addicts, while the addicts learn from them. A place where Christians can discover what addiction is really about, and how best to reach and help people with addictions. Then they can return to their own fellowships to share their insights and prepare a work of discipling and acceptance in their own local area.

INTO THE FUTURE 155

Since becoming a Christian eleven years ago, I have not only seen God's grace at work in my own life but also seen God changing many other people. God is in the restoration business.

NO TIME TO WEEP was first published in 1989. Many who have read the book say the story is unfinished and have asked about Steven and Lyn, so here is an update on family news.

When we first became Christians God told us, through a prophetic message, that he would restore our family. God has kept his promise, not just with close family but with distant relatives too.

On moving to Bristol to work for LFW, Steven, then twenty-one, decided to stay in Brighton. He is still in Brighton, now married to Linda and doing well as a painter and decorator.

Four and a half years ago I came to work for the ELIM HOUSING ASSOCIATION to run an inner city hostel for 45 young, and often vulnerable people; another time of learning. During this period Lyn came from Yorkshire to live with us; another time of family reconciliation, a time where Pat and Lyn got to know each other again. Lots of tears and hugs and inner healing has taken place and their relationship now could not be closer. Saffron is now fifteen and has a good relationship with both Steven and Lyn.

In 1989 Pat's father died of cancer. Three months before he died he came to Bristol to spend time with us and discovered for himself God's love and saving grace.

The years of drug addiction played havoc with our family, yet we both knew that God would bring us together again. Lyn spent three years with us and in September 1993 she married Darren from London. Both Steven and Lyn are now settled, which gave the opportunity for God to re-kindle the vision for a rehabilitation centre in the Bristol area. For the last seven years I have carried with me a promise from God that one day we would run our own centre. There were many times when nothing was happening and I began to doubt if I had heard God properly but God always keeps His promises.

As I write this short family update we are nearing the fulfillment of that promise. This summer of 1994 we are both renewing our friendship with Life for the World and opening the CALEB PROJECT in Clevedon, just eleven miles from Bristol. The CALEB PROJECT is not the fulfillment of my vision, it is only part of what God is doing in our lives and the city of Bristol. As government resources are cut back for drug rehabilitation we are excited by the challenge of the work God is leading us into.

The CALEB PROJECT will be run as an extended family with male and female residents, in partnership with local churches. Both Pat and I believe that people with life controlling problems need to experience the love of Christ in a family atmosphere. We have witnessed God's ability to restore our own family and bring about family healing. We believe that over the coming years we will see many young people come to know Jesus Christ as their Saviour and Healer, as they place their trust and their problems into God's hands.

Please pray for us as we begin a new phase in our calling.

Ron and Pat Norman
March 1994

If you would like information about rehabilitation, to share in this work, or would like Pat and I to come and share our experiences with you, please contact us at the following address:
The Caleb Project, 21 Victoria Road, Clevedon, Avon. BS21 7RU.

Needing help?

If you, or someone you know, wants help to break free from drugs or alcohol, please contact us. If you simply want to talk, we will listen.

Life for the World Trust
Wakefield Building, Gomm Road,
High Wycombe, Bucks HP13 7DJ.
Tel 0494 462008.

Want to help?

Want to know how to help those with addiction problems? If you want to help us in the work of bringing release to drug addicts and alcoholics, please make contact.

Life for the World Trust is a Christian charity involved in a number of drug related projects in cities and towns in the UK and Eastern Europe. We provide residential rehabilitation, together with training for churches and other groups who want to help addicts come to complete freedom.

Please write, or telephone,

Life for the World Trust
Wakefield Building, Gomm Road,
High Wycombe, Bucks. HP13 7DJ.
Tel: 0494 462008.

Charity No. 252054.